Russia and the USSR

1905 to 1991

ALAN WHITE

SERIES EDITOR: CHRISTOPHER CULPIN

Collins
Educational
An Imprint of
HarperCollins*Publishers*

Contents

Unit 1	The downfall of Tsarism	*6*
Unit 2	Lenin's Russia, 1917 to 1924	*16*
Unit 3	Soviet Russia under Stalin, 1924 to 1953	*28*
Unit 4	Khrushchev and Gorbachev	*48*
	Glossary	*60*
	Index	*62*

About this book

This book is about the history of Soviet Russia for History at GCSE. The content is arranged into four units.

On the first page of each unit the book makes clear exactly what you are going to find out about and what key questions the unit will answer.

Then come two or more pages called 'setting the scene'. These give you some of the basic information you will need in order to work through the rest of the unit. You will find these pages useful later if you have to revise this topic for the GCSE examination.

The rest of each unit is called 'issues and enquiries'. These tell you a lot more about the history, topic by topic, but they all have plenty for you to do: investigations to follow up, simulation games and discussions. They also include assessment questions. These are aimed at the assessment objectives for GCSE. You should be able to:

- remember what you have learnt, recall it to mind and then select and organise this information in answer to a question;
- describe what happened in the historical periods and topics you have studied;
- explain why the things you have described were like that and how they happened that way;
- understand how other people explain and interpret the past;
- analyse and use different kinds of historical evidence to find out about the past.

There are plenty of other interesting things in the book – but you'll find out about those when you get to them!

2

Russia and the USSR

1905 - 1991

Introduction

This book is concerned with the beginning and the growth of the Soviet Union until until its collapse in 1991. The Soviet Union is a state which no longer exists. Why study a state which no longer exists?

Most historians would answer that Soviet history is worth studying for its own sake. It is an especially turbulent and disturbing history - to a large extent a history of suffering.

Another answer is that the Soviet Union was the first communist or Marxist state and perhaps the most important. In the 1980s, hundreds of millions of people lived in countries which described themselves as communist or Marxist. An understanding of Marxism and the Soviet Union's history is therefore important to any well-informed person.

A third reason for studying Soviet history is that under Stalin and Khrushchev, the Soviet Union had a PLANNED ECONOMY which is very different from our own. A planned economy is one in which wages, prices and levels of industrial and agricultural production are decided by the government. In Britain, most of these things are left to individuals to decide, with the government playing a much smaller part. Much is to be learnt from a comparison of the two systems.

Studying the Soviet Union under Stalin involves studying the workings of a TOTALITARIAN STATE. In a totalitarian state only one political party is allowed. This party forces its ideas on the rest of society and aims to control all aspects of people's lives. A study of the Soviet Union will help you to understand - in a way that a study of British history cannot - what can happen when a government wields enormous uncontrolled power.

Soviet poster produced on the fifth anniversary of Lenin's death, 1929.▼

THE SAFETY-VALVE.

THE CZAR: *I must relieve the pressure, or —*

▲Steelworks at Magnitogorsk, 1934.

◀'The Safety Valve' – a British cartoon of October 1905.

Map labels:

Kronstadt

Leningrad
(St Petersburg, Petrograd)

Brest-Litovsk

Mogilev

Moscow

UKRAINE

Dneiper
Dam

Simbirsk

Don Basin

Ural Mountains

Ekaterinburg

WESTERN SIBERIA

UNION SOVIET
SOCIALIST REPUBLICS

River Volga

Novocherkassk

Stalingrad
(Volgograd)

Magnitogorsk

Black Sea

River Lena

Baku

Caspian Sea

KAZAKHSTAN

MONGOLIA

CHINA

AFGHANISTAN

N

0   50

km

This book traces the history of Soviet Russia, from its emergence after the 1905 Revolution to its collapse in 1991. The map above shows some of the places referred to in the book. There are other maps, but you may need to refer back to this page as you work through the book.

The map also shows the location of the main industrial areas in Soviet Russia. The industries shown in purple were first developed before 1914, but were further developed under Josef Stalin. Those industries shown in orange were first developed under Stalin during the Five Year Plans.

In addition, the main GULAG labour camps

created by Stalin are shown, as are the 'Virgin Lands' opened up under Khrushchev. You will read more about these aspects of life in Soviet Russia in this book.

By looking at the timeline opposite, you can discover some of the major events in the history of Soviet Russia. You can trace the development of Russia from the end of the autocratic rule of the Tsar at the 1917 Revolution, through Lenin's, Stalin's, Khrushchev's and Gorbachev's times as leaders. You will notice that details are also included of the Russian rulers from 1964 to 1991. This may help to put the period covered by the book into context.

Map legend

KOLYMA

EASTERN SIBERIA

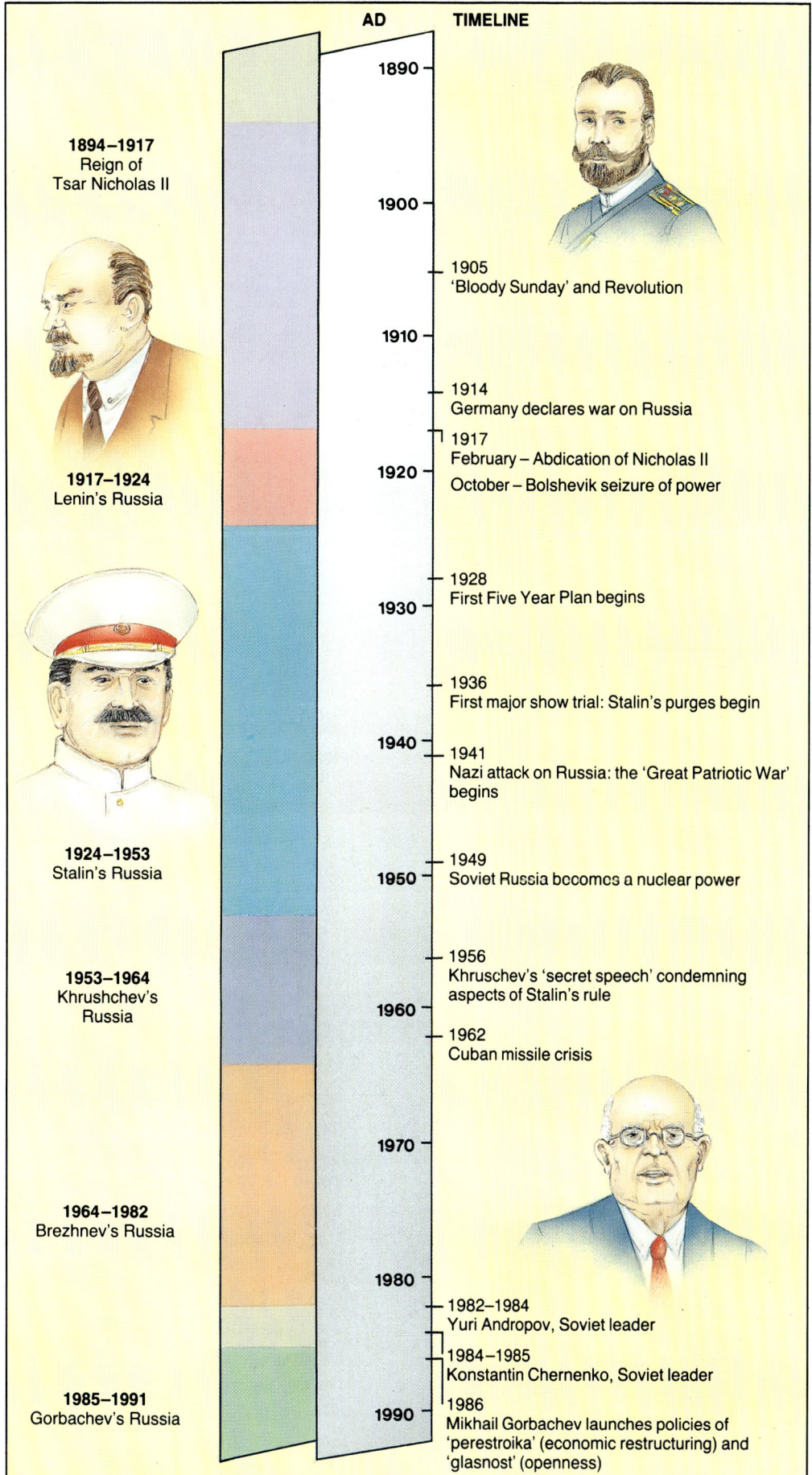

(purple)	Principal locations of GULAG labour camps under Stalin
(orange)	The 'Virgin Lands' opened up under Khrushchev

Industrial areas

(purple)	First developed under Stalin
(orange)	First developed before 1914; further developed under Stalin

Engineering

Iron and steel

Coal

Oil

Timeline

1894–1917
Reign of Tsar Nicholas II

1917–1924
Lenin's Russia

1924–1953
Stalin's Russia

1953–1964
Khrushchev's Russia

1964–1982
Brezhnev's Russia

1985–1991
Gorbachev's Russia

AD   TIMELINE

1890

1900

1905
'Bloody Sunday' and Revolution

1910

1914
Germany declares war on Russia

1917
February – Abdication of Nicholas II

October – Bolshevik seizure of power

1920

1928
First Five Year Plan begins

1930

1936
First major show trial: Stalin's purges begin

1940

1941
Nazi attack on Russia: the 'Great Patriotic War' begins

1949
Soviet Russia becomes a nuclear power

1950

1956
Khruschev's 'secret speech' condemning aspects of Stalin's rule

1960

1962
Cuban missile crisis

1970

1980

1982–1984
Yuri Andropov, Soviet leader

1984–1985
Konstantin Chernenko, Soviet leader

1986
Mikhail Gorbachev launches policies of 'perestroika' (economic restructuring) and 'glasnost' (openness)

1990

The downfall

Nicholas II's Russia:

In 1894 Nicholas II was crowned Tsar of Russia.

What sort of country did he inherit?

Did it deserve its reputation in the rest of Europe as a primitive and backward state?

Soon after Nicholas became Tsar he called suggestions that he should share his power with his people 'senseless dreams'. In 1917 power was taken from him.

Did Nicholas lose power because he was a bad ruler?

Were there forces at work in Russia which any ruler would have been unable to control?

Key Questions

What were the preconditions of revolution in Russia?

What were the triggers of revolution in 1905 and in 1917?

Why did Tsarism survive in 1905 but not in 1917?

Early in 1917, demonstrators crowded on to the streets of Russia's capital. They were protesting against the scarcity and high cost of food. Bread, as Source 1, shows, was in particularly short supply. Demonstrations had happened before. In the past the streets had been cleared by troops. On this occasion, though, some army units refused to obey their officers' orders and instead sided with the demonstrators. Others followed. Within days two things became clear. One was that Russia's Tsar had lost control of the city which was the nerve-centre of his government. The other was that virtually no one was willing to help him regain it. Nicholas II was left with no alternative but to give up his throne. His downfall had come suddenly but it did not come as a surprise.

Nicholas II's Russia was a country in which a privileged few lived lives of luxury while the majority lived in poverty. No one was more privileged than Nicholas himself. Something of the splendour of his court is shown in Source 2. He and his family had an army of fifteen thousand servants to attend to their every need. Much of his time was spent hunting, yachting and playing tennis.

Life for most of Nicholas's one hundred and thirty million subjects was very different. In the Russian countryside the peasantry lived for the most

land of troubles

◄ SOURCE 1
Bread queues in Petrograd, 1917.

▼ SOURCE 2
The coronation of Nicholas II.

▲ SOURCE 3
Factory workers' living quarters in the 1890s.

part in squalid and rat-infested wooden huts. Diseases such as cholera and typhus were rife. Living conditions in the growing industrial towns were, as Source 3 shows, no better.

Nicholas II's Russia was an autocracy. An AUTOCRACY is a state ruled over by one person whose powers are unlimited. The Russian people had no real say in how they were governed. Nor were they allowed to express their political opinions freely. In these circumstances there were many who felt that the only way to change things was through violence.

Some historians who specialise in the study of revolutions make a distinction between what they call the preconditions and the triggers of revolution. Preconditions are problems of a basic kind which make revolution a possibility. Triggers are the events which spark revolution off. The preconditions of revolution were there throughout Nicholas's reign. On two occasions events triggered a revolution off. In 1905 Nicholas survived. In 1917 he did not.

Russia before 1914: economy and society

Nicholas II's Russia had a population and a land area much bigger than those of great powers like Britain and Germany. Russia did not, however, have a strong industrial base, as Source 4 shows, and Russian agriculture was also backward.

The peasants

Before 1914 most Russians were peasants (see Source 5). A peasant is someone who farms land he or she either owns or rents from a landlord. Peasants do not work for employers in return for wages.

In Russia before 1914, farming methods were inefficient. In most villages the land was divided into three large fields. Each household had strips in each of the three fields. One of the fields was left uncultivated each year to allow it to regain fertility. At any one time, therefore, one third of a village's land was not being used to grow crops. Poverty in the countryside was not, however, the result of inefficient farming methods alone. The rapid growth in population which was taking place before 1914 meant a lot more mouths to feed. In addition, taxes were heavy.

Sources 6 and 7 give you some idea of what work and life were like in a Russian village at the turn of the century.

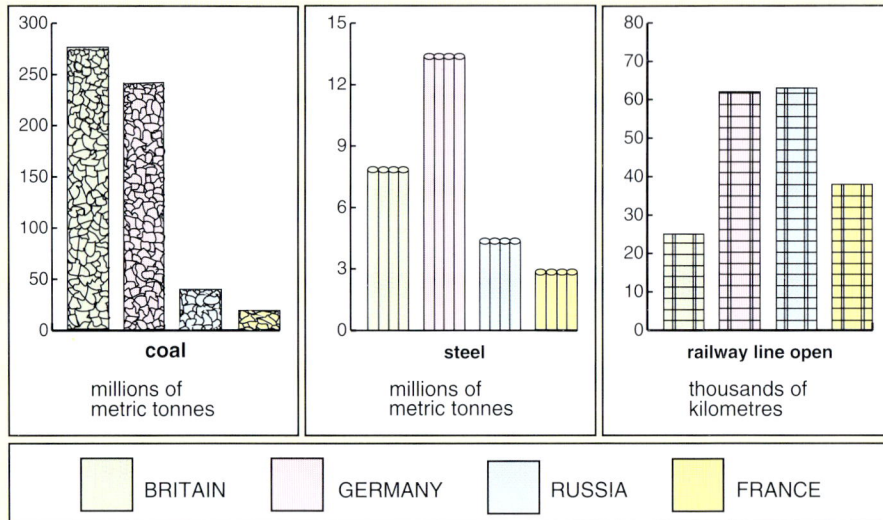

coal
millions of metric tonnes

steel
millions of metric tonnes

railway line open
thousands of kilometres

BRITAIN   GERMANY   RUSSIA   FRANCE

▲ SOURCE 4
The economies of the European great powers in 1914.

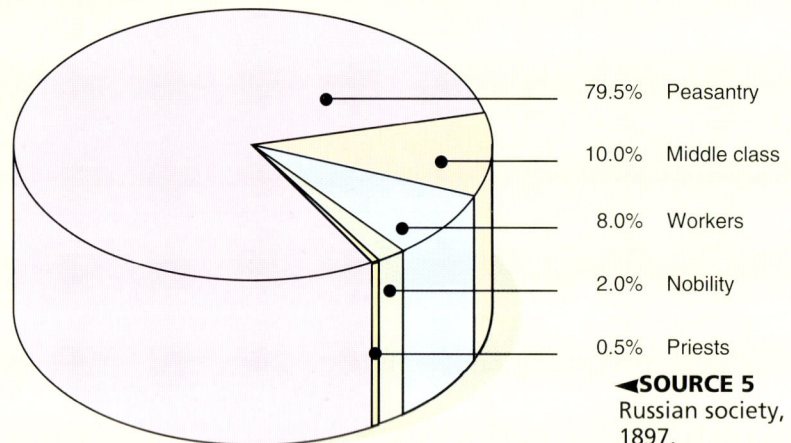

79.5% Peasantry
10.0% Middle class
8.0% Workers
2.0% Nobility
0.5% Priests

◄ SOURCE 5
Russian society, 1897.

SOURCE 6

The wide village street is a sea of liquid mud. Pigs wander up and down the street in search of food. The whole village gives an impression of poverty and squalor.

(A journalist describes life in a Russian village, 1897.)

SOURCE 7 ►
Peasant women hauling barges on the River Volga, 1913.

Land reform

Before 1914 a major attempt at land reform was made by P.A. Stolypin, the Tsar's chief minister from 1906 to 1911. Through his reform, Stolypin hoped to create a prosperous class of peasants who would support Tsarism. It involved peasant households being given their own compact holdings instead of strips scattered across three large fields. In order to create such holdings the power of the *mir* – the peasant councils which organised communal farming – had to be broken. Stolypin called his policy 'a wager on the sober and the strong'. Its impact was limited. By 1914 less than 10 per cent of peasant households were farming compact holdings. Stolypin himself was assassinated in 1911.

Industry

In the 20 years up to 1914 Russian industry began to grow fast.

Industry in Russia did not grow in the way that it had done in Britain. Britain's industrial revolution had come about through the efforts of private businessmen and the government did not get involved. In Russia the growth of industry was planned and promoted by the government.

Like the PEASANTRY, workers in Russia's industries had plenty of reasons for anger and bitterness as Source 8 shows.

SOURCE 8

"The whole day we pour out our blood and sweat. Every minute we expose our life to danger. When there are accidents they accuse us of carelessness. The greed of the bosses, the long working hours, the meagre wages – there is the cause of all accidents.

(From a Russian trade union leaflet, 1898.)"

QUESTIONS

1 Why were Russia's rulers before 1914 so committed to a policy of economic growth?

2 How far did industrial growth benefit the mass of the Russian people?

FOCUS ...*Sergei Witte*

- Born 1849.
- Made his reputation in railway management.
- Nicholas II's Minister of Finance, 1892–1903.
- Tsar's chief minister, 1905–1906.
- Did more than anyone else to promote the development of industry in Russia before 1914.

Sergei Witte was the ablest of all Nicholas's ministers. His aim was a strong and prosperous Russia. He believed that Russia could only remain strong and become prosperous if its industries grew. Witte encouraged foreigners to invest in Russia's industries and tried to protect these industries against outside competition by means of duties on imported goods. He also attached great importance to railway building, believing that railways would bring the different parts of Russia together. In the 1890s over 16,000 kilometres of railway track were laid down. Though a brilliant organiser, Witte had his weaknesses as a politician. He was arrogant and openly ambitious and so made enemies easily. His enemies persuaded Nicholas to dismiss him as Finance Minister in 1903.

Though he was recalled to office briefly in 1905 to 1906, Nicholas no longer really had confidence in him.

The Tsar's opponents

Before 1905 political parties were illegal in Russia. Opponents of Tsarism had to meet in secret. When political parties were made legal in 1905, those opponents of the Tsar who did not believe in the use of force were able to come out into the open. Revolutionaries who were ready to overthrow Tsarism by force could not. Some revolutionaries lived in Russia on the run from the authorities while others lived in exile abroad.

As Source 9 shows, some of the opponents of Tsarism were liberals and others were socialists. What the liberals wanted above all else was a constitution which would limit the Tsar's power and guarantee basic rights, such as freedom of speech. Socialists wanted not only political changes but far-reaching economic changes too. Their aim was a Russia in which private ownership of land was largely eliminated.

▼ **SOURCE 9**
Tsarism's opponents.

LIBERALS

Constitutional Democrats
(or 'Cadets')

Founded: 1905

Support: middle classes

Methods: non-violent

Leader: Paul Milyukov

Ideas: the Cadets wanted to strip the Tsar of virtually all of his power and to turn him into a constitutional monarch. Some wanted to go further and turn Russia into a republic – a country with an elected president, not a monarch.

The Octobrists

Founded: 1905

Support: middle classes

Methods: non-violent

Leader: Alexander Guchkov

Ideas: the Octobrists were more moderate than the Cadets and were satisfied by the promises of limited reform made by the Tsar in his 1905 October MANIFESTO.

SOCIALISTS

Russian Social Democratic Labour Party

Founded: 1898, but in 1903 split into two factions, Bolsheviks and Mensheviks, which went on to become separate parties. Both factions were disciples of Marx (see FOCUS opposite) but disagreed over tactics: the Bolsheviks wanted the Social Democrats to be a tight-knit party of professional revolutionaries; the Mensheviks wanted a party with a broader membership.

Support: working class

Methods: seizure of power by revolution

Ideas: Marxist socialist

Bolshevik leader: Vladimir Lenin

Menshevik leader: Yuly Martov

The Socialist Revolutionaries

Founded: 1901

Support: peasantry

Methods: seizure of power by revolution: in addition, the extremist 'Combat Detachment', led by Evno Azeff, believed in attacking Tsarism by assassinating ministers and officials.

Ideas: the SRs wanted Russia to remain a largely agricultural country in which land was not owned privately but was controlled by each village community. They disliked strong central government and wanted villages to have as much control over their own affairs as possible.

Leader: Victor Chernov

Why was Nicholas II able to emerge from the 1905 Revolution with his powers largely intact?

1905 Revolution

In 1905 Nicholas II's power came under serious challenge. Two events triggered this. Most important was 'Bloody Sunday' (January 1905), when troops opened fire on a crowd of 200,000 people who had gathered outside the Tsar's palace in St Petersburg to present a petition listing their grievances. At least a hundred people were killed and a thousand wounded. The other event was the Russo–Japanese War of 1904 to 1905. Russia and Japan both wanted to expand at the expense of China. Russia suffered a series of crushing defeats, especially at the naval battle of Tsushima (May 1905). The war was a blow to the prestige of Nicholas and his ministers. It made them look foolish and incompetent.

After 'Bloody Sunday' Russia seethed with unrest. There were peasant uprisings in the countryside and a wave of protest strikes in the towns. In St Petersburg and elsewhere factory workers elected a council, or soviet, to co-ordinate protest. One of the leaders of the St Petersburg Soviet was Leon Trotsky. There were also mutinies in the armed forces, most famously on the battleship 'Potemkin'.

Nicholas's initial reaction to these events was confused and indecisive. Eventually, as Source 10 suggests, he was forced to act. He did so with some skill, taking advantage of the fact that his peasant, working-class and middle-class opponents made no attempt to work together. In his October Manifesto, Nicholas offered to create a parliament (Duma) with limited powers. He said that in future he would share responsibility for making laws with the Duma. This offer split and weakened middle-class liberals. Working-class protest was crushed by force: the St Petersburg Soviet was disbanded and its leaders exiled. The leaders of the peasant uprisings were treated brutally too: hundreds were hanged on the orders of P. A. Stolypin, the Tsar's new chief minister. In the countryside the hangman's noose became known as 'Stolypin's necktie'.

Once Nicholas had regained power he made sure that the Duma he had been forced to create had little real power. He continued to think and act like an autocrat.

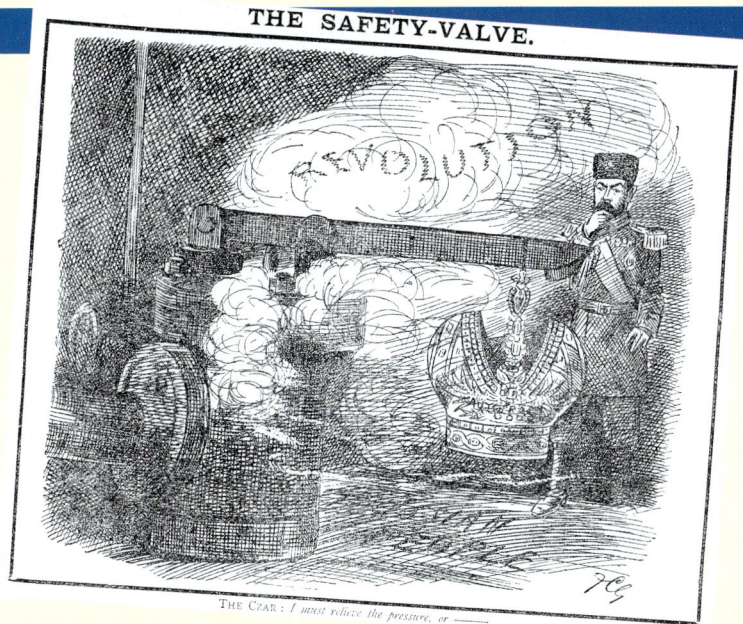

THE SAFETY-VALVE.

THE CZAR: *I must relieve the pressure, or —*

▲ **SOURCE 10**
'The Safety Valve' – a British cartoon of October 1905.

FOCUS ...*Karl Marx*

- Born 1818; died 1883.
- Political philosopher of German origin who lived much of his life in Britain.
- Major books: *The Communist Manifesto* (1848) and *Capital* (1867).

Marx believed that history was shaped by struggles for power between different SOCIAL CLASSES. He argued that the growth of industry had produced conflict between the capitalist class, the BOURGEOISIE, and the landowners who had dominated the rural or 'feudal' societies which existed before industrialisation. After the bourgeoisie had defeated the landowners, claimed Marx, there would be a conflict between the capitalists and the PROLETARIAT, the industrial workers. The workers, increasingly poor and desperate as a result of exploitation, would rise in revolt and destroy the bourgeoisie. Following their revolution, the workers would create a communist society. Note that in Marx's view successful workers' revolts could only occur in industrial societies – not in largely rural ones like early twentieth century Russia.

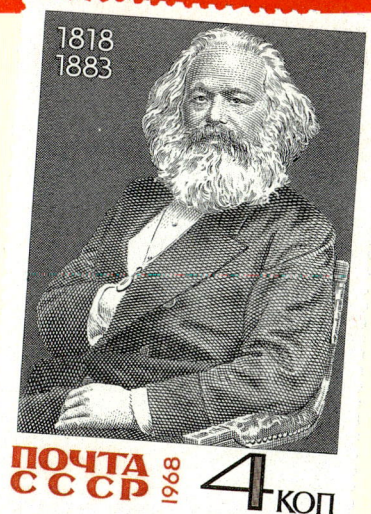

1818 1883

ПОЧТА СССР 1968 4 КОП

The First World War and the downfall of Tsarism

How did the First World War affect Russia?

During the First World War hostility towards Tsarism within Russia became deeper and more widespread than it had been in 1905. Look at Sources 11 and 12. Nicholas II was viewed with contempt by all sections of society.

The middle classes and the war
The Russian middle classes were deeply patriotic. In 1914 they looked forward to the destruction of Germany's armies. They were to be bitterly disappointed. In 1914 Russia's armies suffered heavy defeats in the battles of Tannenberg and the Masurian Lakes (see Source 13). During 1915 the Germans drove deep into Russian territory. In 1916 a major counter-attack was launched under General Brusilov but no lasting gains were made.

SOURCE 11

Everybody was fed up with the Tsar because they thought he was weak. When he ABDICATED there was great rejoicing everywhere. My parents opened champagne bottles and celebrated with friends.

(Margot Tracey, daughter of a Russian industrialist, remembering 1917.)

SOURCE 12

We must speak of a movement of acute and profound resentment against the person of the currently reigning emperor. All the recent happenings have intensified this mood to a terrifying degree. This is as much the mood of the middle classes as it is of the lower classes.

(From a secret police report, 1916.)

▼ **SOURCE 13**
Map of Russia at war, 1914–1917.

The last major Russian military offensive was launched by General Brusilov on 4 June 1916 and lasted for three months. It took four hundred thousand prisoners but failed to reach Lublin or Lemberg, its objectives.

German victories 1914

Russian territory occupied by the central powers 1914-1915

The middle classes, angry and frustrated, blamed the Tsar for the failure of Russia's war effort. Nicholas II was certainly a feeble and incompetent war leader. He made perhaps his biggest mistake in 1915 when he decided to take charge of Russia's forces, leaving the capital, Petrograd (the wartime name for St Petersburg), to direct operations from army headquarters at Mogilev, near the front.

The decision by Tsar Nicholas to leave Petrograd had damaging consequences. It meant that the Tsar was liable to be blamed personally when battles were lost. It also meant that his wife, the Tsarina, Alexandra, was left in day-to-day control of affairs in Petrograd. As a German, Alexandra was unpopular with the Russian people. She was also under the influence of a MYSTIC, Grigory Rasputin, believing him to be capable of controlling the illness (HAEMOPHILIA) from which her son suffered. The Tsarina allowed Rasputin to exercise considerable power in politics (see Source 14). Sources 15 and 16 give some indication of the feelings prevalent in Russia in the middle years of the First World War. Rasputin was murdered in 1916, but by then the damage to Tsarism had been done.

> ## SOURCE 14
>
> The influence of Rasputin on the Tsarina, which affected through her the entire policy of the government, grew to fantastic limits. One need only recall the ministerial leapfrog. From the autumn of 1915 to the autumn of 1916, there were five ministers of internal affairs and four ministers of agriculture. There was confusion, there were contradictory orders, there was no firm will, no decisiveness, no single definite policy for victory.
>
> (From the memoirs of Mikhail Rodzianko, a leading Octobrist, published in 1926.)

SOURCE 15

We have many reasons for being discontented with the government. But all the reasons boil down to one general reason: the incompetence and evil intentions of the present government. This is Russia's chief evil, and victory over it will be equal to winning an entire campaign.

(P. A. Milyukov, Cadet leader, speaking in 1916.)

◄ **SOURCE 16**
'The Russian Royal House' – a Russian cartoon of 1915 showing Nicholas, Alexandra and Rasputin.

The peasantry and the war

The First World War was not a total disaster for Russia's peasants. In one way they gained from it: after 1914 they were able to get higher prices for the food they produced. For the most part, though, the war meant misery for peasant households. There were four main reasons for this:

- The impact of CONSCRIPTION: most of the 14 million Russian men called up to serve in the army between 1914 and 1917 were peasants.

- Heavy casualties: nearly two million Russian soldiers were killed and six million were either wounded or taken prisoner between 1914 and 1917.

- The loss of so many young men to the army meant that much farm work had to be done by women and by the elderly.

- Consumer goods, like boots and cloth, became scarce and expensive.

By 1916 the peasantry were tired of war. The Russian novelist Bunin wrote in that year that the peasantry no longer wanted to fight: 'They don't understand what we are fighting for. The war isn't their business. They grow more furious every day.'

The war-weariness of the peasantry did not, however, pose as serious a threat to Tsarism as middle-class or working-class discontent. The peasantry was scattered across Russia, far from the centre of government.

Assessment

1 Suggest three ways in which the First World War contributed to the downfall of Tsarism.

2 Of the ways you have suggested, which do you think was the most important? Give reasons for your answer.

3 Which of the reasons for the downfall of Tsarism go back to before 1914?

4 'The First World War was the main reason for the downfall of Tsarism.' How far would you agree with this view?

5 To what extent was Nicholas II responsible for his own downfall?

Petrograd and its workers, February 1917

The working class and the war

In the towns the war meant rapidly rising prices. There were several reasons for this. Harvests were low during the war years because some important food-producing areas fell into enemy hands. In this time of uncertainty there was HOARDING by the peasantry. The railway system became so clogged up with military traffic that food supplies did not always find their way into the towns. Source 17 shows how quickly prices rose in the war years. The impact that rising prices had on working-class families is shown in Sources 18 and 19.

Revolution, February 1917

In February 1917 crowds gathered in the centre of Petrograd. They shouted slogans like 'Give us bread!', 'Down with the government!' and 'Down with the war!'. Rioting broke out. Units of the Petrograd GARRISON mutinied, refusing to charge the crowds (Source 20). The Tsar, marooned at army headquarters near the front, was powerless. He ordered that the rioters be shot, but his orders were not carried out. There were very few armed men left in Petrograd who could be relied upon to act against the rioting crowd.

The Tsar ordered the Duma to stop meeting, but its members ignored his instructions. Ministers and officials deserted their posts and the Tsar's government fell apart. Russia's army commanders persuaded the Tsar to abdicate. The formalities were completed in a railway siding at Pskov, 320 kilometres from Petrograd (see Source 21).

The revolution of February 1917 was not masterminded by liberal politicians or by professional revolutionaries. It was the workers and soldiers of Petrograd acting on their own initiative who brought Tsarism down. If the Tsar had been able to rally support elsewhere in Russia he might have been able to regain control of Petrograd. By 1917, though, he had no support left.

SOURCE 17		
Wages and prices in Petrograd, 1914 and 1917 (in roubles)	**1914**	**1917**
Monthly wage, unskilled worker	20	50
Monthly wage, skilled worker	40	80
Bag of potatoes	1	7
Bag of flour (16 kg)	3	16
Pair of boots	6	30

SOURCE 18

The economic condition of the masses is worse than terrible. The impossibility of buying many food products and necessities and the increasing incidence of disease due to malnutrition and unsanitary living conditions – cold and dampness because of a lack of coal and wood – have made the workers ready for the wildest excesses of a hunger riot.

(From a secret police report about Petrograd, 1916.)

SOURCE 19

Resentment is felt worse in large families, where the children are starving. Mothers, exhausted from standing endlessly at the tail of queues, are stockpiles of flammable material, needing only a spark to set them afire.

(From a secret police report about Petrograd, 1917.)

SOURCE 20
Soldiers join the revolution, February 1917.

Provisional Government

There was no ready-made government to replace that of the Tsar. The right to rule until a new CONSTITUTION could be drawn up was claimed by the middle-class liberals who dominated the Duma. They formed a Provisional Government (see Source 22) in which the leading figures were the Cadet leader Milyukov (Foreign Minister) and the Octobrist leader Guchkov (War Minister). Prince Lvov, a respected but not forceful ARISTOCRAT was made Prime Minister. He, however, was only a figurehead and had no real power. The only socialist in the Provisional Government was Alexander Kerensky, a lawyer, who became Minister of Justice. Kerensky was invited to join the Provisional Government because Milyukov and the others thought he was popular with the Petrograd workers. Kerensky belonged to a political group called the Trudoviks: they were allies of the Socialist Revolutionaries.

The Provisional Government was handicapped from the outset by the fact that it was not in control of Petrograd. After the Tsar's abdication, power in the capital lay in the hands of the Petrograd Soviet – a council of 3,000 workers and soldiers representing factory workers and army units stationed in Petrograd. Each member of the Soviet represented roughly a thousand workers or soldiers. How long each member served on the Soviet was up to the factory or army unit he represented. The membership of the Soviet was constantly changing. In the spring of 1917, the Petrograd Soviet was dominated by the Mensheviks and Socialist Revolutionaries.

For a time the Mensheviks and Socialist Revolutionaries were prepared to allow the Provisional Government to run the country. Their attitude changed in May 1917 when Milyukov declared that Russia would remain at war until Germany had been defeated. There was uproar in Petrograd. The Petrograd Soviet called Milyukov's declaration 'absolutely unacceptable'. The Socialist Revolutionaries and the Mensheviks, anxious for peace, forced the middle-class liberals out of the Provisional Government and took control of it themselves.

▲ SOURCE 21
The abdication of Nicholas II, February 1917.

▲ SOURCE 22
The Provisional Government, March 1917. Most of the ministers were Cadets.

QUESTIONS

1 *At what point in the years between 1900 and 1917 did Nicholas II's downfall become inevitable? Give reasons for your answer.*

2 *Of the sources on pages 12 to 15 which are the most important in showing the mood of:*

   – the working class?
   – the middle class?

   Which source is the most useful to a historian?

Lenin: statesman

When Lenin arrived back from exile at Petrograd's Finland Station in 1917 he was the leader of a small and apparently unimportant revolutionary group. Little was known about him either in Russia or abroad.

Within months Lenin and the Bolsheviks had seized power in Russia. In this unit we will find out how this happened. We will go on to see what kind of rule Lenin established in Russia.

Key Questions

How and why were the Bolsheviks able to seize power in October 1917?

How much did the Bolsheviks' success owe to Lenin's leadership?

Why were the Bolsheviks able to survive and to consolidate their rule?

How did revolution change Russia up to 1924?

Without Lenin, Russia would almost certainly not have become a communist state. If Russia had not become a communist state, COMMUNISM would almost certainly not have established itself in eastern Europe and elsewhere in the world after 1945. Lenin is therefore one of the key figures of twentieth-century world history. He is also one of the most controversial.

One of Lenin's great achievements was the October Revolution. In the early part of 1917 few in Russia could have thought that a Bolshevik seizure of power was possible. For one thing, the Bolsheviks had only a small following in Russia – much smaller than that of the Socialist Revolutionaries (see Source 9 on page 10). Also, the Bolsheviks were a Marxist party, and Marxists believed that successful communist revolutions could only take place in advanced industrial societies. For this reason, some Bolsheviks in Russia in 1917 believed that no attempt should be made to seize power.

On his return to Russia from exile in the spring of 1917, Lenin brushed the doubters aside. He insisted that a bid for power could succeed and set about building a base from which it could be launched.

Source 1 is a Soviet artist's

or tyrant?

◄ SOURCE 1
Lenin
approaching
Finland Station,
Petrograd, 1917.

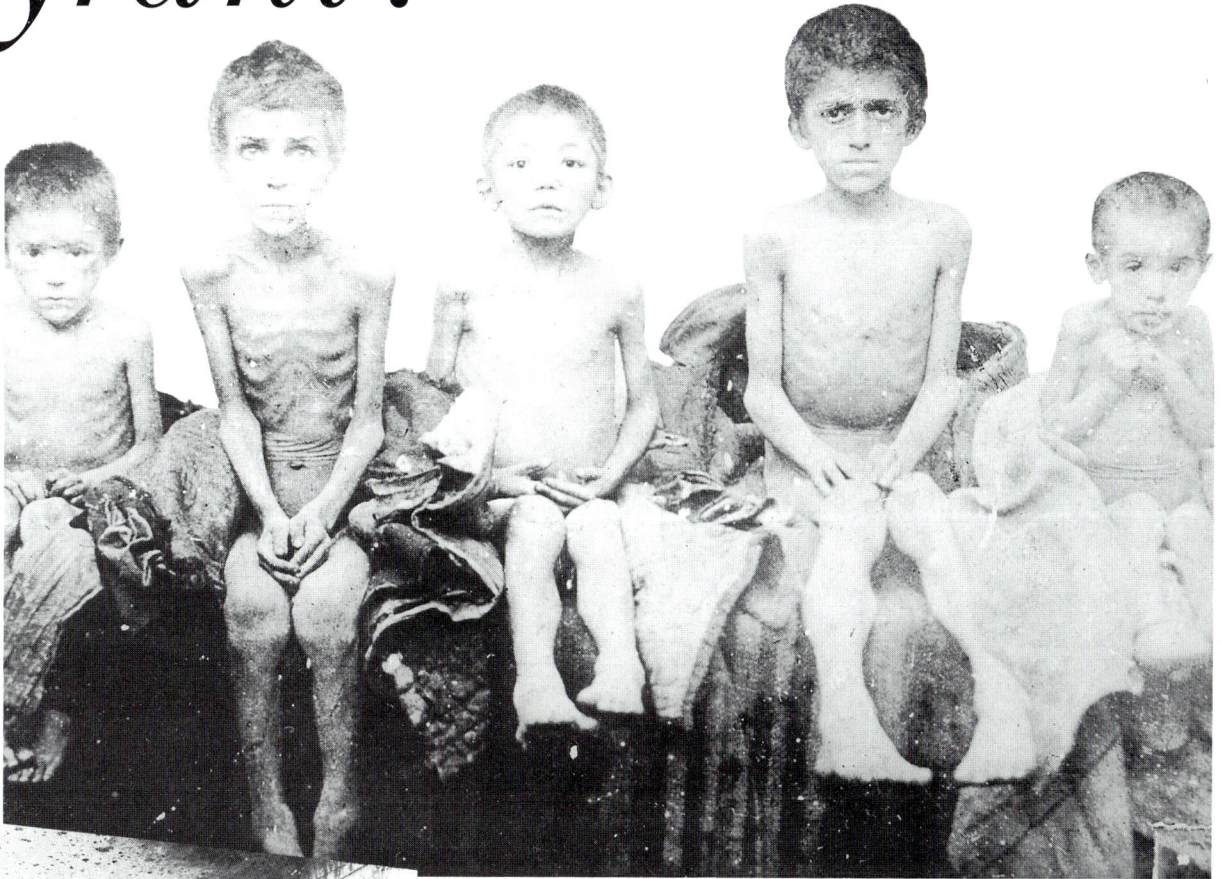

◄ SOURCE 1
Lenin
approaching
Finland Station,
Petrograd, 1917.

SOURCE 2 ►
Famine victims,
1921.

▲ SOURCE 3
A Bolshevik
execution cell in
Kiev. The marks on
the wall are
bloodstains.

view of Lenin's return to Russia. By the autumn of 1917 even Lenin's enemies did not deny that he was daring and resourceful.

Another of Lenin's great achievements was to hold on to power after he had seized it. This was, if anything, a greater achievement than seizing it in the first place. The first years of the infant Bolshevik state were extremely difficult. The Bolsheviks had to battle with a series of enemies – Germany, the 'White' Russians, Tsarist Russia's wartime allies and the new state of Poland. Within the territory they controlled, the Bolsheviks faced persistent problems of disorder and food shortages. In the conflicts which followed their seizure of power, the Bolsheviks became notorious for their ruthless methods. Were these the only methods that could have been used? Sources 2 and 3 provide some idea of the depths to which Russia descended at this time.

In the years after 1917 Lenin, openly and without apologising, used methods of terror and intimidation. Did he do so only because the circumstances left him with no alternative? Or was he a fanatic who did not care about human suffering? It is a point on which Lenin's admirers and critics disagree.

Lenin's Russia 1917 to 1924

After the Bolsheviks seized power in October 1917, one of Lenin's main priorities was to end the war with Germany. The Germans had taken advantage of Russia's weakness and had made big gains. They were in a position to demand a high price for the peace Lenin wanted. In March 1918 the Bolsheviks, after much debate, agreed to the Treaty of Brest-Litovsk. Large amounts of territory, industry and population were surrendered to the Germans in exchange for peace (see Source 4). Later, after Germany's defeat in the war, Russia was able to regain control of some of this territory.

After Brest-Litovsk, civil war broke out in Russia in earnest. The Bolsheviks' enemies – the 'White' Russians – received support from Tsarist Russia's wartime allies. During the civil war, the Bolshevik heartland was a large area of western Russia centred on Moscow. The Bolsheviks made Moscow their capital in mid-1918 because Petrograd was too open to attack. Source 5 shows from where and by whom this heartland was threatened.

Russia lost:
- 20% of its railways
- 33% of its factories
- 75% of its iron and steel capacity
- 62 million people

Territory surrendered by Russia

▲ SOURCE 4
Map showing what Russia surrendered after the Treaty of Brest-Litovsk, March 1918.

Time chart

Political

1917 (Oct.) Bolshevik seizure of power.

1917 (Nov.) Election of the Constituent Assembly.

1917 (Dec.) Formation of CHEKA.

1918 (Jan.) Dissolution of Constituent Assembly.

1918 (March) Treaty of Brest-Litovsk. Bolsheviks adopt the name Communist Party.

1918–1920 Civil war.

1918 (July) Murder of royal family.

1920 Russo–Polish war.

1921 Treaty of Riga with Poland.

1924 (Jan.) Lenin's death.

Science and technology

1920 State Commission for the Electrification of Russia established to put into practice Lenin's slogan 'Communism equals Soviet power plus the electrification of the whole country.'

Economic and social

1918 (June) Nationalisation of oil, textile, mining and metallurgical industries as part of the 'War Communism' policy.

1921–1922 Famine.

1921 (March) Introduction of the New Economic Policy (NEP).

Cultural and religious

1918 (Jan.) 'Decree on the separation of the church from the state and the school from the church.'

1917 onwards – Artists Chagall, Kandinsky and Rodchenko at work in Russia.

1922 Patriarch (head) of the Russian Orthodox Church imprisoned.

1922 'Glavlit' set up to censor literature.

Lenin in power

During the Civil War Russia was in a chaotic condition. Output in industry and in agriculture sank to disastrously low levels (see Source 6). However, there was some recovery after the war: Source 6 also shows this. This recovery was thanks to the New Economic Policy (see pages 24–25).

The organisation which Lenin and the Bolsheviks set up to govern Russia after the October Revolution was called the Council of People's COMMISSARS ('Sovnarkom' in Russian). Lenin became its chairman. Trotsky was at first Commissar for Foreign Affairs, then became Commissar for War. Stalin was Commissar for Nationalities. An important body attached to the Council of Peoples Commissars was the Vesenkha or the Supreme Economic Council. This was formed in December 1917. Its job was to organise economic life in the new Bolshevik state.

Output of Russian industry and agriculture
(in millions of tonnes)

	1913	1921	1924
coal	29.5	9.0	16.4
iron	4.3	0.1	0.7
steel	4.3	0.2	1.1
grain	81.4	38.2	52.2

▲ **SOURCE 6**
Output of Russian industry and agriculture, 1913 to 1924.

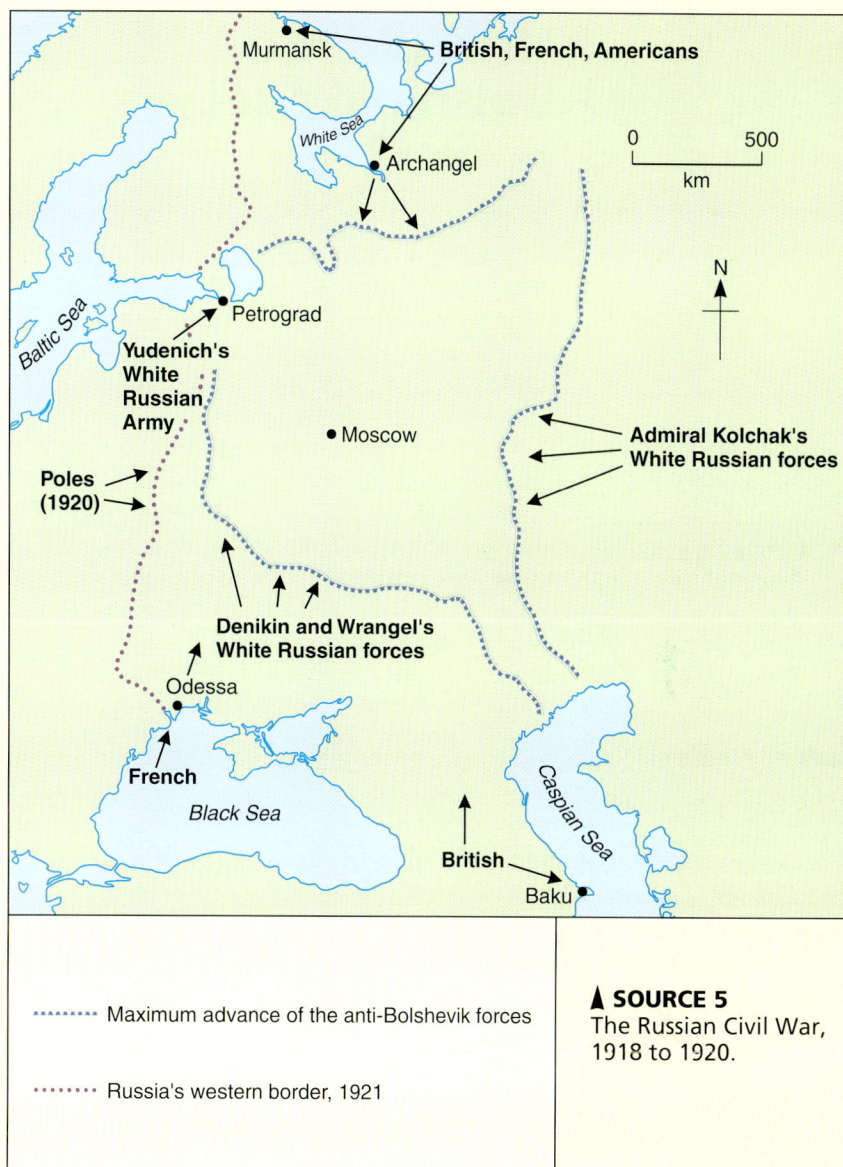

.... Maximum advance of the anti-Bolshevik forces

······ Russia's western border, 1921

▲ **SOURCE 5**
The Russian Civil War, 1918 to 1920.

FOCUS ...*Lenin before 1917*

- **Born 1870.**
- **Real name Vladimir Ulyanov.**
- **Spent most of his adult life in exile from Russia.**

Born into a middle-class family at Simbirsk, 800 kilometres west of Moscow, Lenin was a committed revolutionary from his late teens onwards. A formative experience was the execution in 1887 of his older brother, Alexander, for his part in an assassination attempt on the Tsar.

Lenin was first arrested when he was 20. He graduated in law at St Petersburg University while living 1,600 kilometres away. In the late 1890s he was exiled to Siberia for three years. Between 1900 and 1917, with the exception of two years in Russia from 1905 to 1907, he lived in exile in western Europe – in Germany, Britain, France and Switzerland.

He returned to Russia with German help in 1917. This gave rise to accusations by his enemies that he was a German spy.

How did the Bolsheviks seize power?

At the time of Lenin's return to Russia in the spring of 1917 the political scene was dominated by the Socialist Revolutionaries and the Mensheviks. Alexander Kerensky, an ally of the Socialist Revolutionaries and deputy chairman of the Petrograd Soviet, became Prime Minister of the Provisional Government. Kerensky and his colleagues saw their task as looking after things until a democratically elected government was installed. Source 7 shows the sequence of events they hoped would take place.

Lenin's intentions

Lenin had no intention of allowing this sequence of events to unfold. His aim was to seize power. He did not want democratic elections to take place because he knew the Bolsheviks would lose. His slogan was 'All power to the Soviets'. Lenin thought the Bolsheviks would be able to win control of the important Petrograd Soviet.

In mid-1917 Lenin knew that the Bolsheviks had to build up their strength before they could launch a serious bid for power. His plan for attracting new support for the party, set out in his 'April Theses', involved trying to exploit the frustrations which existed in the army and among the peasantry.

In 1917 the Russian army was disintegrating (see Sources 8 and 9). Its soldiers wanted an end to the war. The Provisional Government, however, wanted them to fight on until a peace settlement involving not only Russia but also her allies – Britain, France and the United States – could be agreed upon. Lenin promised that if he got into power he would immediately make a separate peace with Germany.

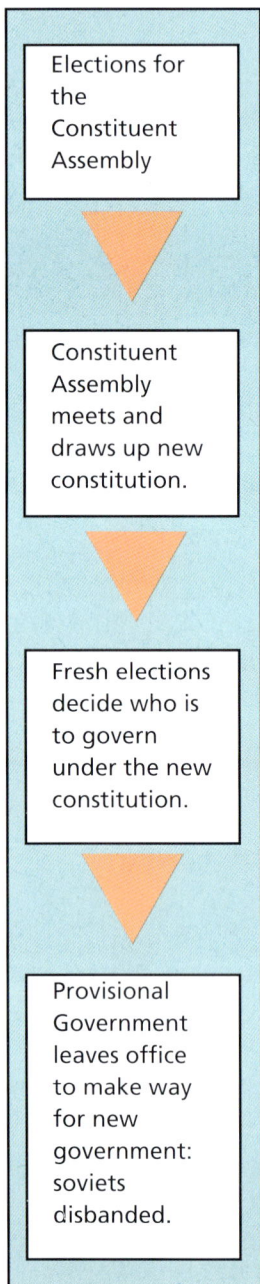

Elections for the Constituent Assembly

▼

Constituent Assembly meets and draws up new constitution.

▼

Fresh elections decide who is to govern under the new constitution.

▼

Provisional Government leaves office to make way for new government: soviets disbanded.

◄ SOURCE 7
The sequence of events expected by Kerensky's Provisional Government.

SOURCE 8

"Desertions continue unabated. Discipline declines with each passing day. The authority of officers and commanders has collapsed. A pacifist mood has developed in the ranks.

(From a Russian general's report on the mood in the Russian army, mid-1917.)"

SOURCE 9 ►
A Russian soldier attacking two deserters, 1917.

In 1917 peasants, taking advantage of the confusion in Russia, began to seize land belonging to people who owned large estates. The Provisional Government called upon them to stop, claiming that land reform was a matter which had to wait for a properly elected government. Lenin urged the peasants on with his slogan 'All land to the peasantry'.

The 'July Days'

By July 1917 support for the Bolsheviks had grown. Kerensky, unable to make peace or to halt rising prices, was unpopular. Big street demonstrations took place in Petrograd (see Source 10). Lenin hesitated. Although Bolshevik agitators were prominent in these demonstrations, Lenin stopped short of calling for the overthrow of Kerensky.

Instead, Kerensky struck at the Bolsheviks, ordering the arrest of their leaders. Lenin fled to Finland. The 'July Days' were a disaster for the Bolsheviks.

The Bolshevik revival

In late 1917 the Bolsheviks regained their strength. This was largely due to a botched attempt at a military takeover by General Kornilov, the commander-in-chief of the army. He wanted to overthrow the Provisional Government and restore order in Russia. When he ordered troops to march on Petrograd, they were persuaded to turn back by Bolshevik factory workers – 'Red Guards' – sent out to meet them. In addition, Bolshevik railway workers refused to allow Kornilov to make any use of the rail network.

After Kornilov's failed bid for power, the Bolsheviks were able to claim that they had saved the country from counter-revolution. Their popularity in Petrograd soared. They won a majority in the Petrograd Soviet. Leon Trotsky, a recent convert to the Bolshevik ranks, became president. By now Kerensky was an isolated figure. It was widely rumoured in Petrograd that he had been in league with Kornilov.

It was clear to Kerensky at this point that a Bolshevik attempt to seize power was about to happen. He left Petrograd in order to try to drum up support elsewhere. This made things easy for the Bolsheviks. Trotsky drew up a plan to take control of Petrograd. Little resistance was

▲ SOURCE 10
The 'July Days', 1917.

SOURCE 11

The Bolsheviks were a pure usurpation, the real Russia was wholly against them, the elections everywhere would go against them and they dared hold none.

(Kerensky, talking to a British journalist, early in 1918.)

encountered when the Bolsheviks acted on the night of the 24–25 October 1917.

In Moscow things did not go so smoothly: it only fell to the Bolsheviks after a week of heavy fighting. Kerensky's reaction to events can be seen in Source 11.

QUESTIONS

1 **In what ways did Lenin display political skill in 1917?**

2 **How justifiable are Kerensky's comments in Source 11 on the unpopularity of the Bolsheviks?**

Why did the Bolsheviks win the Civil War?

The Bolsheviks' success in the Civil War of 1918 to 1920 was partly the result of their own skill and ruthlessness and partly the result of their enemies' weaknesses. One of the Bolsheviks' main assets was Lenin's ability to take hard decisions. The best example of this in the Civil War period was the treaty with Germany in 1918: Lenin paid the high price for peace demanded by the Germans even though many Russians were outraged. He also paid a high price for peace when Russia was attacked by the new state of Poland in 1920. Initially, the Soviet army beat the Poles back, but it then suffered a heavy defeat in the battle of Warsaw (August 1920). Under the Treaty of Riga (1921) Russia surrendered 130,000 square kilometres of territory to Poland.

Trotsky's contribution to the Bolshevik cause was almost as important as Lenin's. When civil war came, Trotsky quickly fashioned the Red Army into an effective fighting force. His methods though, and those of the Red Army, were brutal in the extreme (as described in Sources 12 and 13).

Felix Dzerzhinsky

Another important contributor to the Bolsheviks' victory was a Polish Communist named Felix Dzerzhinsky (Source 14). Dzerzhinsky was head of the Extraordinary Commission for the Struggle Against Counter-Revolution, Sabotage and Speculation (Cheka). The Cheka was responsible for the 'Red Terror' which began in 1918 and was only relaxed when the Civil War ended. Anyone suspected of opposition to the Bolsheviks was shown no mercy (refer back to Source 3 on page 17).

The Whites

The weaknesses of the White Russian forces were numerous. There were different

> ## SOURCE 12
>
> The position of officers of the old Tsarist army in the Red Army is painful in the extreme. Mobilised for service but mistrusted, they are shot for the least failure of their troops. By a recent order of Trotsky's the wives and children of officers who desert to the Whites are thrown into prison.
>
> (From a British intelligence report, 1918.)

> ## SOURCE 13
>
> Right from the start the Red Army killed all the White officers they took prisoner. They shot them or they cut their medals off and gouged out their chests.
>
> (From the memories of George Novikoff, a White Russian soldier, late 1980s.)

▼ **SOURCE 14**
Felix Dzerzhinsky.

FELIKS DZIERŻYŃSKI
95 ROCZNICA URODZIN
60 GR
POLSKA
1877 – 1972
Z. STASIK   PWPW-72

groups among them – Mensheviks, Socialist Revolutionaries, Cadets and officers of the old Tsarist army – who found it hard to co-operate. Their armies were in different parts of the country – Siberia, the Ukraine and the Baltic area – and co-ordination was difficult. The reputation of the White armies for savagery was as bad as that of the Bolsheviks. A major weakness was the belief among the peasantry that if the Whites won they would lose the land they had seized in 1917. Source 15 is an analysis of the strengths and weaknesses of the Bolsheviks and the Whites.

The Whites were also open to the charge that they were being used by foreign powers (see Source 16). Foreign intervention in Russia's affairs began after the Treaty of Brest-Litovsk. The treaty alarmed Russia's wartime allies because it allowed Germany to transfer large numbers of troops from Russia to the Western Front in France. The Allies sent aid to the Whites in the hope that the Bolsheviks would be replaced by a government which would go back to war with Germany. They also sent troops to Russia – about 100,000 in all – but these did little serious fighting.

▲ SOURCE 16
Bolshevik poster showing the Whites and the Allied Powers: the dogs are (left to right) Denikin, Kolchak and Yudenich.

> SOURCE 17

Of all the tyrannies in history, the Bolshevik tyranny is the worst, the most destructive, the most degrading. The atrocities committed under Lenin and Trotsky are incomparably more hideous and more numerous than anything for which the Kaiser is responsible.

(Winston Churchill, then British Secretary for War and Air, 1919.)

After the war
After the ARMISTICE of November 1918 brought the war with Germany to an end, Allied troops remained in Russia even though the original motive for intervention had gone. They did so for a variety of reasons: anger over the 'Red Terror' in general and over the murder of the royal family (at Ekaterinburg in Siberia in 1918) in particular, fury over Lenin's refusal to pay the Tsar's foreign debts and, in some cases, hatred and fear of Bolshevism (see Source 17). Also, the Allied governments did not want Bolshevik ideas to spread among their own working classes. However, after November 1918, the Allied intervention was a half-hearted affair. By 1920 virtually all Allied troops had been withdrawn.

Assessment

1 *What can you tell about the methods used by the Bolsheviks to win the Civil War from Sources 12 and 13?*

2 *Which do you think is the more useful of the two sources?*

3 *Taking its origins into consideration, assess the reliability of Source 15 as evidence of the state of opinion in Russia in 1918.*

4 *'Not a reliable source about the Whites or the Allies, but a valuable source nevertheless': how far would you agree with this comment on Source 16? Give reasons for your answer.*

5 *If you were to base your view of the Bolsheviks' rule during the Civil War on Sources 12, 13 and 15 alone, could you be sure that your view would be a fair and accurate one?*

From War Communism to the New Economic Policy

What effects did the Civil War have on Russia? What changes did Lenin make to deal with its effects?

During the Civil War Lenin concentrated his energies on the business of running the Russian economy. He had to ensure that the Red Army was fed and equipped. This meant keeping the factories of Petrograd, Moscow and other cities at work. It also meant squeezing an adequate supply of food out of the peasantry.

Lenin's answer to this was a policy of 'War Communism'. Industries were put under state control and military-style discipline was imposed in the factories. Trade unions were brushed aside. In the towns there was a system of food rationing. Soldiers and industrial workers received most food, members of the middle class the least. In the countryside, the government was ruthless. Peasants were reluctant to sell grain because Russia's paper money was almost valueless and there were few CONSUMER GOODS to buy: the Bolsheviks responded by taking grain from them by force. Sources 18 and 19 show the effects of the Bolsheviks' policy.

> **SOURCE 18**
>
> People were starving. Snow everywhere. The trams had stopped. Rationing had been brought in.
>
> (A Bolshevik Party member, Augustus Karlovich, describing Moscow in 1920.)

▲ **SOURCE 19**
Food requisitioning: a White Russian poster.

SOURCE 20▶
'Long Live the Red Navy – Vanguard of the Revolution': a Bolshevik poster of 1920.

State of revolt

The peasantry responded to grain REQUISITIONING with violence. By 1921, whole provinces of Soviet Russia were in a state of revolt. Then the Bolsheviks faced a challenge from another quarter. The sailors of Russia's Baltic fleet, based at Kronstadt, had been among the Bolsheviks' most fervent supporters in 1917. After the October Revolution they were openly praised and flattered by the Bolshevik regime (see Source 20). In 1921, however, disillusioned by Bolshevik ruthlessness and ever-worsening conditions, the Kronstadt sailors rose in rebellion against Bolshevik rule. Thousands were killed when the Red Army suppressed the rebellion. Opposition of this ferocity from people he had once described as 'the pride and glory of the revolution' left Lenin badly shaken.

The New Economic Policy

Lenin responded to the crisis of 1921 by abandoning War Communism in favour of the New Economic Policy (NEP). The New Economic Policy had three main features:

- The requisitioning of grain was stopped. Under the New Economic Policy, peasants had to hand over some of their grain in the form of a 'tax in kind' but they were able to sell what was left over.

- Heavy industry and the transport system remained under state control.

- Free enterprise was to some degree restored in other sectors of industry. Many small factories were returned to the owners and consumer goods were produced and sold for profit.

Lenin described the NEP as a 'retreat'. It was a retreat which enabled the Bolsheviks to overcome a serious threat to their authority and which prevented a breakdown of economic life in Russia. The Russian economy began to revive under the new policy (see Source 6 on page 19). The NEP also led to the emergence of a class of profit-driven merchants and traders known as 'nepmen' (Source 21). This angered some Bolsheviks (see Sources 22 and 23). The return to private enterprise which Lenin permitted went against their socialist principles. Lenin, however, would not tolerate protest. He banned the formation of separate groups or factions within the Party. What was now expected from ordinary party members was unquestioning obedience.

SOURCE 21
Nepmen at work in Smolensk market, Moscow, 1921.

SOURCE 22

There wasn't a scrap of food in the country. We were down to a quarter of a pound [114g] of bread per person. Then suddenly they announced the NEP. Cafes started opening, restaurants. Factories went back into private hands. It was capitalism. In my eyes what was happening was the very thing I'd struggled against.

(Leonid Orlov, Bolshevik supporter, remembering the introduction of the NEP, late 1980s.)

SOURCE 23

In 1921 we used to discuss the NEP for hours on end at Party meetings. Most people supported Lenin. Others thought he was wrong. Many even tore up their party cards.

(Nikolai Izachik, Bolshevik Party member, recalling the introduction of the NEP, late 1980s.)

Assessment

1 **What changes did the New Economic Policy bring to:**

   a) *economic life in Soviet Russia?*

   b) *political life in Soviet Russia?*

2 **What remained unchanged by the introduction of the New Economic Policy?**

3 **Who gained, and who lost, from the introduction of the NEP?**

4 **In what ways did Soviet Russia change from 1917 to 1921?**

Lenin: interpretations

What has been said about him?

Lenin's death

Vladimir Ilyich Lenin died in January 1924 aged 53. He had been in poor health since an assassination attempt in 1918: Fanya Kaplan, a Socialist Revolutionary, shot him twice from close range, one bullet entering his neck, the other his lung. In 1922 Lenin suffered the first of a series of strokes and from that time onwards it was clear that he was dying. He continued to work but his role became less and less influential.

The 'Lenin cult'

After Lenin's death, a 'Lenin cult' developed in Soviet Russia. His image was everywhere – in statues, plaques and posters (see Source 24). Petrograd was renamed Leningrad in his honour. Some loyal Communists in the 1920s even christened their newborn daughters 'Ninel' – Lenin spelt backwards.

Lenin's body was not buried but was embalmed and put on display in a specially built MAUSOLEUM in Moscow's Red Square. The mausoleum became a place of pilgrimage for the Communist faithful (see Source 25).

The 'Lenin cult' survived for as long as Soviet Russia itself. In the 1940s a biography of Lenin, written in Russia, called him 'the greatest genius of all times and of all nations, master of all the treasures of human knowledge'. Placards on the streets in Russian cities in the 1960s declared: 'Lenin is more alive than all those living now.' What would Lenin himself have made of the cult?

During his lifetime, he disliked personal adulation and tried to put a stop to it. For this reason his wife, Krupskaya, opposed the Lenin cult after his death. In 1924 she wrote in the newspaper *Pravda*: 'Do not build memorials to him, name palaces after him, do not hold magnificent celebrations in his memory. All of this meant so little to him.' She was ignored.

Early interpretations

Assessments of Lenin's career produced in the 1920s within Soviet Russia, and by Communist sympathisers outside Russia,

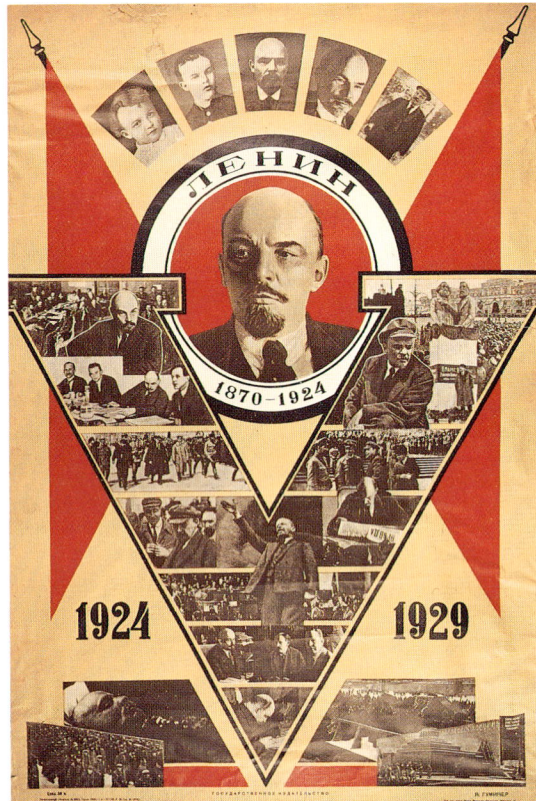

◄ **SOURCE 24**
Soviet poster produced on the fifth anniversary of Lenin's death, 1929.

SOURCE 25 ►
Lenin's mausoleum depicted by the cartoonist David Low, 1932.

SOURCE 26

"A fearless mind, a will of iron, a burning hatred of slavery and oppression, a revolutionary passion that moved mountains, boundless faith in the creative energies of the masses, vast organisational genius.

(Lenin's qualities as described by the Bolshevik Party's Central Committee, January 1924.)"

were reverent in tone. Source 26 is an example. Assessments produced by anti-Communist writers were very different. Anti-Communists were blind to Lenin's achievements. Instead they drew attention to the murderous activities of the Cheka and the murders of the Tsar and the royal family. The U-turn of 1921 when Lenin permitted a return to free enterprise in order to cling on to power was also emphasised (see Source 27).

Recent interpretations

What have later twentieth-century historians made of Lenin? Remember that more recent interpretations can take a more detached view of things than writers in the 1920s. As Source 28 shows, there is a wide measure of agreement on certain points. Controversy, however, remains. It centres on the question of Lenin's responsibility for the way in which Soviet Russia developed after his death. Lenin's critics say that he paved the way for the horrors of the Stalin era by using methods of terror and by creating, after 1921, a climate of opinion inside the Communist Party in which differing views could not be aired openly. Lenin's defenders reply that the resort to violence and terror was forced upon him. In other words, Lenin was not a ruthless dictator. They also point to the way in which Lenin, at the end of his life, tried to remove Stalin from power. Sources 29 and 30 are the views of two British writers.

SOURCE 27

Lenin was one of the most sinister and sombre figures that ever darkened the human stage. This evil man was the founder and mainstay of Bolshevism. It is a great mistake to look upon him as a moderate. He was a revolutionary whose thirst for blood could never be quenched. Mistaken ideas about him have arisen because he tempered his fanaticism with political cunning. He saw that men must at times have some breathing space.

(From the *Morning Post*, a British newspaper, January 1924.)

SOURCE 28

Almost all writers agree Lenin was a great political leader. Usually there is full agreement that Lenin was quite unscrupulous in the means he used to promote his policies and attain his ends. Almost all historians recognise his modesty, lack of vanity, absence of personal ambition.

(Walter Laqueur, historian, writing in 1967.)

SOURCE 29

We must realise that the violent zigzags in Soviet policy in the years after 1917 were caused by desperate temporary necessities: we must not allow them to confuse our estimate of Lenin's purpose. In the Russia of 1918 to 1920 ... when we recall that a very large number of civil servants had deserted their posts or stayed only to spy and sabotage, it appears quite miraculous that the machinery of the state functioned at all, and we are better able to appreciate the sometimes crude methods which perforce had to be adopted in this period of War Communism.

(Christopher Hill, historian and Marxist, writing in 1947.)

SOURCE 30

It is possible to absolve Lenin from total responsibility for the ruin caused by the numerous military campaigns, but not from the unnecessary suffering and wastage caused by War Communism. And during the conflict with external enemies Lenin was strengthening the internal apparatus of COERCION, establishing a one-party state and dispensing with more moderate forms of socialist democracy. In the process he demolished one of history's more promising 'might have beens'.

(Stephen Lee, historian and liberal, writing in 1987.)

Assessment

1 Refer back to Sources 2, 12, 13 and 22. How do you think the authors of Source 26 might have used this evidence to support their interpretation of Lenin?

2 How do you think the author of Source 27 might have used the same evidence to support his or her interpretation?

3 Do you agree that the interpretation presented in Source 29 is closer to the truth than that contained in Source 30?

4 Do you think the interpretations of Lenin presented in each of Sources 26, 27, 29 and 30 are likely to have been influenced by the political views of the authors who produced them?

5 Do you think it is likely that an account of Lenin's rule with which all historians agree will ever be produced? Give reasons for your answer.

Terror, war and

In this unit we shall see that Josef Stalin, though a prominent Bolshevik from 1912, was not thought of by his colleagues as a future leader. In the early 1920s he seemed an anonymous figure, best suited to routine administrative work. His nickname was 'Comrade Card Index'. By 1929, however, Stalin had established himself as undisputed dictator of Soviet Russia. We shall see that in the 1930s Stalin's government waged war on its people – first when agriculture was collectivised, then in the 'Great Terror'.

Russians who survived the 1930s faced, in 1941, a further threat to survival – the Nazi invasion. Stalin became Russia's war leader. We shall end by seeing how effective a war leader he was.

Soviet Russia was transformed under Josef Stalin. To begin with there was an economic transformation. Stalin set out to turn Soviet Russia into a major industrial power within a very short space of time. He succeeded: substantial economic gains were made. They were advertised to the Soviet people and to the wider world by means of giant prestige projects like the Moscow metro, the steel city of Magnitogorsk and the Dnieper dam (Source 1). The industrial base built under Stalin in the 1930s was strong enough, when war came, to beat off and then to defeat Nazi Germany. Stalin's economic achievements were, however, bought at great cost to the Soviet people. Millions lost their lives when agriculture was collectivised. Could these achievements have been brought about by methods other than the brutal ones employed by Stalin?

Totalitarian state

Under Stalin, Soviet Russia was also transformed politically. Stalin's Russia was a totalitarian state. In a totalitarian state, the ruling party forces its beliefs on the rest of society and tries to

Key Questions

How was Stalin able to establish himself as dictator in the Soviet Union?

What was his dictatorship like?

How was the Soviet Union transformed under Stalin?

How did the Second World War affect Russia?

▲ **SOURCE 1**
The Dnieper Dam under construction during the first Five Year Plan.

personality cult

stop people from holding other beliefs. Opposition – actual or potential – is dealt with harshly. Stalin's Russia was, among other things, a POLICE STATE in which people could be imprisoned in labour camps (see Source 2) or executed without a trial. Despite the 1936 constitution, described by Stalin as the most democratic in the world, it was a state in which citizens were denied basic liberties, such as freedom of speech.

Soviet Russia was not the only totalitarian dictatorship in Europe in the 1930s. Nazi Germany was also a state of this kind. In Nazi Germany, though, Hitler was not glorified personally in quite the way that Stalin was in Russia. In Russia, posters and statues of Stalin were everywhere (see Source 3). Towns were named after him – Stalingrad, Stalino, Stalinabad. Art and literature was only permitted if it glorified Stalin and his revolution. This 'personality cult', as it came to be known, was contrary to Marxist principles. Marxists believe that history is shaped by economic forces and that the role of the individual is unimportant.

SOURCE 3
Soviet poster glorifying Stalin.

SOURCE 2 ▶
Abandoned labour camp in the Arctic Circle.

The leadership struggle of the 1920s

When Lenin fell ill in 1922 the leading Bolsheviks in Soviet Russia – the members of the party's Political Bureau, or 'Politburo' for short – said that they would operate a system of COLLECTIVE LEADERSHIP between themselves. Stalin, however, had no intention of becoming part of a system of collective leadership. He was as power-hungry as it is possible to be. Even before Lenin died in 1924, Stalin had set about the task of winning power for himself.

At the end of his life, Lenin – realising something of Stalin's true character and ambitions – tried to warn his fellow Bolsheviks against him. In 1923 he added a note to his 'Political Testament' of 1922 – a document in which he had commented on the strengths and weaknesses of leading Bolsheviks – suggesting that Stalin should be demoted (see Source 4). The warning had no effect. Lenin's 'Political Testament' had unflattering things to say about all the Politburo members and they therefore agreed after his death not to make it public.

Stalin versus Trotsky

Stalin's most formidable rival in the 1920s was Leon Trotsky, the ablest of the leading Bolsheviks after Lenin himself. Trotsky and Stalin were men whose background and experiences before 1917 were very different (see fact file below). Their political profiles in 1917 and after differed too. Trotsky organised the seizure of power in Petrograd in October 1917 and went on, as Commissar for War, to create the Red Army. Stalin was less well known. He held two jobs apart from his post as Commissar for Nationalities. In 1919 he was appointed head of the Workers and Peasants' Inspectorate (or 'Rabkrin'), an organisation set up by the Bolsheviks to root disloyal officials out of the civil service. In 1922 he was appointed Secretary-General of the Communist Party.

Stalin had a reputation as both a man of action and a good organiser. He was certainly ruthless in crushing nationalist uprisings during the Civil War.

SOURCE 4

Stalin is too rude ... a fault insupportable in the office of Secretary-General. I propose to COMRADES that they find a way to remove Stalin from that position and appoint to it another man who is more tolerant, more loyal, more considerate and more attentive to comrades.

(Lenin, writing in 1923.)

	TROTSKY	STALIN
Born	1879	1879
Real name	Lev Bronstein	Josef Djugashvili
Nationality	Russian	Georgian
Background	Middle class (father a farmer)	Working class (father a shoemaker)
Education	Odessa University	Secondary school
Early life	In exile abroad 1902–1905 and 1907–1917	In exile in Siberia or on the run from the authorities in Russia: abroad only briefly
Political record	Only committed himself to Bolsheviks in 1917; previously had links with Mensheviks	A committed Bolshevik from 1903 onwards

The 'troika'

During 1923 and 1924 Stalin engineered a dispute with his rival on a point of political doctrine. Trotsky took the view that communism in Russia could never be entirely secure unless there were communist revolutions in other countries (see Source 5). Stalin's view was that a communist society could be established in Russia without revolutions elsewhere (see Source 6). These views were labelled 'permanent revolution' and 'socialism in one country' respectively. The gap between the two views is not as wide as it might appear but it suited Stalin to exaggerate it. Stalin was backed in his dispute with Trotsky by Kamenev and Zinoviev (see FOCUS below). The three of them were known as the 'troika'.

The 'troika' inflicted a decisive defeat on Trotsky at the Thirteenth CONGRESS of the Soviet Communist Party in 1924. Stalin kept a low profile as Zinoviev launched an attack on Trotsky. Not that speeches made much difference: Stalin had ensured that his supporters were in a majority at the Congress. After 1924, Trotsky's fall was swift. In 1925 he was forced to resign as Commissar for War. In 1926 he was expelled from the Politburo. In 1927 he was thrown out of the Communist Party. In 1929 he was expelled from Russia. In 1940 Trotsky was murdered in Mexico by one of Stalin's agents.

SOURCE 5

Without the direct support of the European working class we cannot remain in power and turn our temporary domination into lasting socialism.

(Trotsky on 'permanent revolution'.)

SOURCE 6

"Socialism in one country means the possibility of the working class assuming power and using that power to build a complete socialist society in our country without the victory of working-class revolutions in other countries.

(Stalin on 'socialism in one country'.)"

QUESTIONS

1 *Look again at Source 4. In what ways was Lenin disillusioned with Stalin in 1923?*

2 *How do you think the backgrounds of Stalin and Trotsky before 1917 help to explain their support for 'socialism in one country' and 'permanent revolution' respectively?*

FOCUS ...*Kamenev and Zinoviev*

Lev Kamenev (real name: Rosenfeld)

- Both opposed the idea of a Bolshevik bid for power in October 1917.
- In the mid-1920s both supported Stalin's idea of 'socialism in one country' against Trotsky's emphasis on 'permanent revolution'.
- Both then sided with Trotsky against Stalin on the question of the speed of industrial growth.
- In 1936 both were put on trial on Stalin's orders and both were executed.

Lev Kamenev and Gregory Zinoviev sometimes appear to be the Siamese twins of revolutionary Russia – their names always crop up together. In fact, they were men of different character. Zinoviev was an effective orator of the rabble-rousing kind but was vain and lacked economic understanding. After the October Revolution he became Communist Party boss in Petrograd and was head of the Comintern, the organisation through which Soviet Russia tried to bring about communist revolutions in other countries. Kamenev was an abler and more modest man. Like Stalin, he was a Georgian by origin. After the October Revolution, he became Communist Party boss in Moscow.

Gregory Zinoviev (real name: Radomysylsky)

The leadership struggle: second and third phases

After the defeat of Trotsky, the second phase of the 1920s power struggle opened. Stalin turned on his former allies in the 'troika'. Kamenev and Zinoviev had become impatient with the New Economic Policy. They called for an end to private enterprise farming and insisted on the need for rapid industrialisation. Supporting them was the discredited Trotsky. Together, the three were referred to by Stalin's followers as the 'Left Opposition' (see Source 7). Stalin, backed by Bukharin (see FOCUS below), accused the 'Left Opposition' of recklessness. Bukharin claimed that the NEP had been successful and should be allowed to continue. Kamenev and Zinoviev soon found themselves isolated. By 1927 both men had been relieved of their posts of responsibility.

The third and last phase of the leadership struggle saw the defeat of Bukharin. Stalin did a U-turn in 1928 and 1929, abandoning his support for the NEP and beginning to argue for a policy of rapid industrialisation. He became a more extreme SUPERINDUSTRIALIST than members of the 'Left Opposition' had been. Bukharin and his supporters – chief among whom were Rykov, chairman of the Council of People's Commissars, and Tomsky, head of the trade unions – were routed. They were labelled the 'Right Opposition' by Stalin's

supporters. Bukharin was forced off the Politburo in 1929. The Politburo was now packed with Stalin's henchmen – men like Vyacheslav Molotov and Lazar Kaganovich.

On 21 December 1929 Stalin celebrated his fiftieth birthday. He did so as Soviet Russia's unchallenged leader. The power struggle in which he had been successful is summarised in the chart opposite.

▲ **SOURCE 7**
'We play, but nobody comes to us' – a Russian cartoon showing the 'Left Opposition': Trotsky (organist), Zinoviev (singer) and Kamenev (parrot).

F⬤CUS ...*Nikolai Bukharin*

- **Born 1888; executed 1938.**
- **Editor of *Pravda*, the Communist Party newspaper, and one of the Party's leading economic thinkers.**
- **Described by Lenin as 'a most valuable and major theorist' and as 'favourite of the whole Party'.**

Like Lenin and Trotsky, Bukharin was born into a middle-class family. His parents were Moscow schoolteachers. He came to prominence in 1917 as an extreme left-wing Bolshevik who opposed the Treaty of Brest-Litovsk. He then became, in Bolshevik terms, a moderate. In the mid-1920s he was, of all the leading Bolsheviks, the strongest supporter of the NEP. He shocked some Communists with his call to the peasantry: 'Enrich yourselves'. For all his ability, Bukharin was in some ways politically naive and was no match for Stalin when the power struggle entered its last phase in the late 1920s.

The power struggle of the 1920s: a summary		
Years	Main participants	Apparent reason for conflict
1923–1925	Trotsky versus the 'troika' (Stalin, Kamenev, Zinoviev)	'Socialism in one country' versus 'permanent revolution'
1926–1927	The 'Left Opposition' (Trotsky, Kamenev, Zinoviev) versus Stalin and Bukharin	Speed of industrial growth
1928–1929	The 'Right Opposition' (Bukharin, Rykov, Tomsky) versus Stalin	Speed of industrial growth

Reasons for Stalin's success

Why was Stalin able to defeat his opponents with comparative ease? There are several reasons:

- Stalin's command over the apparatus of the Communist Party enabled him to 'pack' key meetings with supporters.

- There was widespread suspicion of Trotsky within the Communist ranks. One reason was that he had been a Menshevik. Also, past revolutions – such as the French revolution – had ended in military dictatorship. Trotsky, creator of the Red Army, was the Bolshevik leader who seemed most like a Napoleon Bonaparte. Also, Trotsky was not the kind of man who inspired affection. He was aloof and arrogant. He did not bother to hide his contempt for the more dull-witted and ill-mannered people within the Party.

- Trotsky was a loyal member of the Communist Party. Whatever some people may have believed, he never thought of using the Red Army against the Party. At the Thirteenth Congress Trotsky said: 'My party – right or wrong... I know one cannot be right against the Party.'

- Stalin was underestimated by his opponents. They thought he was what Trotsky called him in the 1930s – a mediocrity. He was, in fact, a skilful political intriguer (see Source 8).

SOURCE 8

Stalin is an unprincipled intriguer who subordinates everything to the preservation of his own power. He changes his theory according to whom he needs to get rid of... Our potential forces [those of the Right Opposition] are vast but the middle ranking members of the Party do not understand the depth of the disagreements, and there is a terrible fear of a split. Stalin has made it difficult for us to attack him.

(Bukharin, speaking in private, 1928.)

QUESTIONS

1 Do you think Source 7 was produced by a supporter or by an opponent of Stalin? Give reasons for your answer.

2 Do you think the 'Left Opposition's' policy would have gained the support of the Russian people?

3 How do you think the posts occupied by Stalin in the early 1920s might have helped him to 'pack' meetings with his supporters?

4 Of the reasons given on pages 30 to 33 for Stalin's success in the power struggle of the 1920s, which do you think was the most important?

5 To what extent does Source 8 offer support for the suggestion that Bukharin was politically naive?

The Soviet economy transformed

Why did Stalin abandon the New Economic Policy?

Stalin's decision to abandon the New Economic Policy and to embark on a programme of state-controlled industrialisation is not in itself surprising. After all, the NEP meant capitalism. Industrialisation, so Communists thought, would create a large, politically reliable working class. What is more difficult to explain is why the NEP was abandoned so abruptly and completely.

Two things appear to have influenced Stalin's attitudes. One was the 'war scare' of 1927. On flimsy evidence – the emergence of a right-wing government in Poland and a breakdown in diplomatic relations with Britain – Stalin concluded that the capitalist powers were once more preparing to intervene in Soviet affairs. Sources 9 and 10 reveal something of Stalin's subsequent thinking.

The other thing which influenced Stalin was the grain procurement crisis of 1927 to 1928. Peasants kept grain off the market, hoping that by doing so they would force up prices. Stalin seems to have concluded that the power of the peasantry to hold the state to ransom in this way had to be broken. Another motive for collectivisation was a desire to boost production by replacing the antiquated strip-farming system with one in which modern farm machinery could be used. Also, grain output had to be increased to enable industrial workers to be fed and to finance industrialisation. If this was done by kulaks (richer peasants), then a strong anti-Bolshevik class would emerge in the Russian countryside.

The collectivisation of agriculture

A crash programme for the collectivisation of agriculture was started in 1929. On so-called 'collective' farms, or 'kolkhozy', peasant farmers did not cultivate their own strips of land but farmed all the land available in co-operation with their neighbours. In theory, they then shared the profits they made: in practice, collectivisation meant that the peasants became state agricultural workers. The free market which existed under the NEP was ended: only the state could buy a kolkhoz's produce. This meant that the state could decide what peasants' incomes were going to be. The only thing the peasants could call their own on the kolkhoz was the private plot each household received to enable it to grow food for its own consumption.

In the 1920s the Communists had experimented with state farms ('sovkhozy'), on which there were no private plots. Workers on a sovkhoz were simply paid a wage like factory workers.

Stalin claimed that the mass of the peasantry favoured collectivisation and that only greedy and selfish kulaks opposed it. Sources 11, 12 and 13 show the difference between government claims and reality. When massive resistance was encountered, Stalin said that it came from 'ideological kulaks' – peasants who were not kulaks but who thought like them.

> ## SOURCE 9
>
> The history of the old Russia consisted in being beaten again and again because she was backward. If you are backward and weak you may be beaten and enslaved. But if you are powerful, people must beware of you. We are 50 to 100 years behind the advanced countries. We must make up this gap in 10 years. Either we do this or they crush us.
>
> (Stalin, speaking in 1931.)

> ## SOURCE 10
>
> One of the most important projects was the creation of a heavy industrial base in the Urals and Siberia out of the reach of any invader, and capable of supplying the country with arms and machines in immense quantities.
>
> (John Scott, an American worker in Russia in the 1930s.)

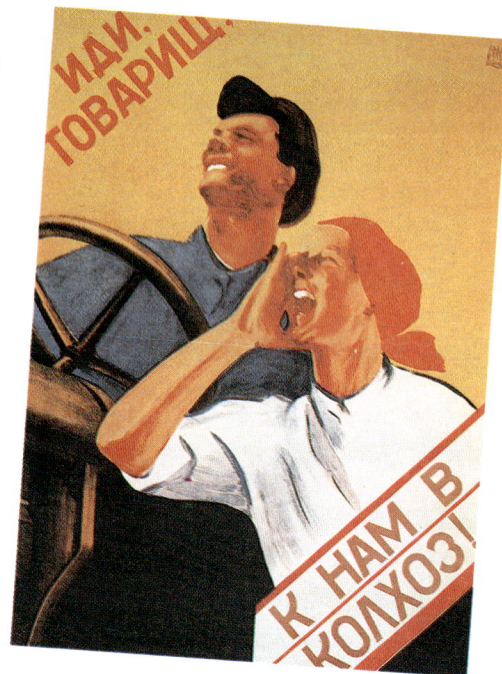

▲ **SOURCE 11**
Soviet poster, 1930: 'Come and join our collective farm, comrade!'

Завершить коллективизацию сельского хозяйства

54

ПРАВЛЕНИЕ КР-ОКТЯБРЬСКОЙ % АРТЕЛИ КОЛХОЗА имени ЦВИЛЛИНГА

... «Дальнейший процесс коллективизации представляет процесс постепенного всасывания и перевоспитания остатков индивидуальных крестьянских хозяйств колхозами.

Это значит, что колхозы победили окончательно и бесповоротно».

◄**SOURCE 12**
Government poster, 1930, calling on the peasants to complete the process of collectivising agriculture.

SOURCE 13

Millions of peasants, rather than give up their livestock to the collectives without compensation, preferred to kill and eat their cows, pigs, sheep and chickens. Many even slaughtered their horses out of sheer indignation. For a brief period Russia ate more meat than it had eaten in decades. Then it went on a vegetarian diet.

(Hubert Knickerbocker, American newspaper reporter in Soviet Russia, writing in 1930.)

Human cost

The human cost of collectivisation was immense. Peasants were not going to give up their land and livestock voluntarily, so villages had to be collectivised by force: TERRORISM and mass murder were carried out by OGPU (the state security police) and by 'Red Guards' sent out from the towns. In 1930 peasant resistance was so fierce that Stalin called a temporary halt to collectivisation, blaming local communist officials for becoming 'dizzy with success' – for being over-zealous.

In 1931 the collectivisation drive was re-started. By 1937 over 90 per cent of peasant households had been collectivised.

One of the purposes of collectivisation was to introduce modern machinery. Such machinery was made available to collective farms by a network of Machine Tractor Stations. These tractor stations also had a political purpose: always staffed by loyal Communists, they were the means by which Stalin's government kept watch on the countryside.

The short-term results of collectivisation were disastrous. As Source 14 shows, agricultural output slumped. In 1932 and 1933 there was a famine. Stalin, though, got much of what he wanted. As millions died of famine, Stalin continued to export grain to earn foreign currencies. The peasantry was no longer a political threat. 'It took a famine,' said a Communist official in 1933, 'to show them who is master here.'

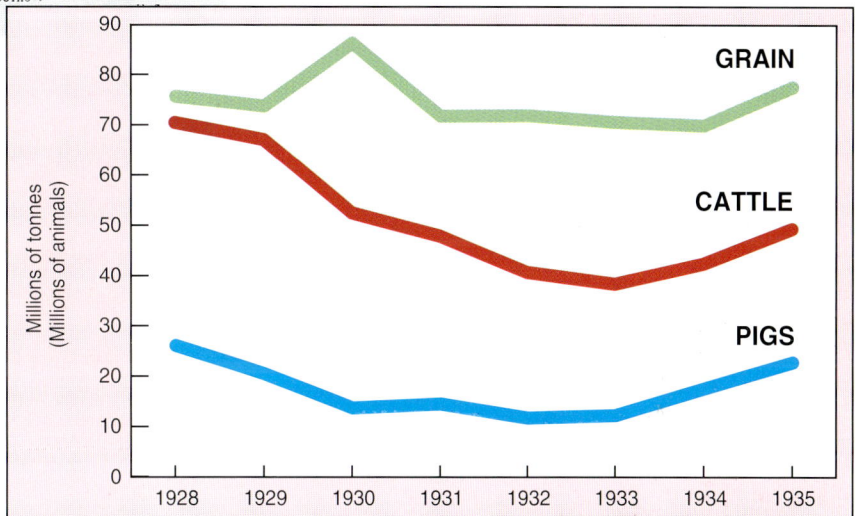

▲ **SOURCE 14**
Soviet agriculture, 1928–1935

Assessment

1 **What do Sources 9 and 10 tell us about Stalin's motives for rapid industrialisation?**

2 **How useful are Sources 13 and 14 for telling us about the failures of the collectivisation programme? Which do you think is more useful?**

3 **Assess the reliability of Sources 11, 12 and 13 as evidence of peasant attitudes to collectivisation.**

4 **What do Sources 11 and 12 tell us about government PROPAGANDA?**

Industrialisation

How was industrialisation carried out, and how effective was it?

In 1928 Stalin embarked on an industrialisation drive described by Britain's ambassador to Soviet Russia at the time as 'the greatest industrial experiment ever tried by mankind'. Stalin's experiment was based on economic planning. In a planned economy prices, wages and production levels are decided by central government and not, as they are in a FREE MARKET ECONOMY, by the forces of supply and demand. In Stalin's Russia, responsibility for detailed planning of the economy lay with the 'Gosplan', the State Planning Commission.

Five-Year Plans

'Gosplan' drew up a series of Five-Year Plans (First: 1928 to 1932; Second: 1933 to 1937; Third: 1938 to 1942) which laid down targets for the Soviet economy to meet. The targets tended to be over-ambitious (as Source 15 shows), but it is clear that the output of Soviet HEAVY INDUSTRY increased dramatically in the 1930s.

Industrialisation under Stalin saw the expansion of Soviet Russia's established industrial areas – Moscow, Leningrad, the Don Basin and Baku. It also saw the creation of new industrial centres, notably the Urals – Kuznetsk coal and steel complex, the centrepiece of which was the Magnitogorsk steel works (Source 16). Source 17 reveals something of what building the Magnitogorsk works involved.

SOURCE 15 Output of Soviet heavy industry 1928 to 1937 (millions of tonnes)					
	1928 Output	**1932** Output (planned)	**1932** Output (actual)	**1937** Output (planned)	**1937** Output (actual)
Coal	36	76.2	65.3	155	130
Iron	3.4	10.2	6.3	16.3	14.7
Steel	4.0	10.6	6	17.3	18
Oil	1.7	22.4	21.7	47.5	29

▼ **SOURCE 16**
Steelworks at Magnitogorsk, 1934.

SOURCE 17

The big whistle sounded a long, deep, hollow six o'clock. All over the scattered city-camp at Magnitogorsk, workers rolled out of their beds and bunks. It was January 1933. The temperature was in the neighbourhood of 35 degrees below. It was two miles to the blast furnaces over rough ground. It was a varied gang, Russians, Ukrainians, Tartars, Mongols, Jews, mostly young and almost all peasants of yesterday. Khaibulin, the Tartar, had never seen a staircase, a locomotive or an electric light until he had come to Magnitogorsk a year before. Now he was building a blast furnace bigger than any in Europe.

(John Scott, an American worker in Russia in the 1930s.)

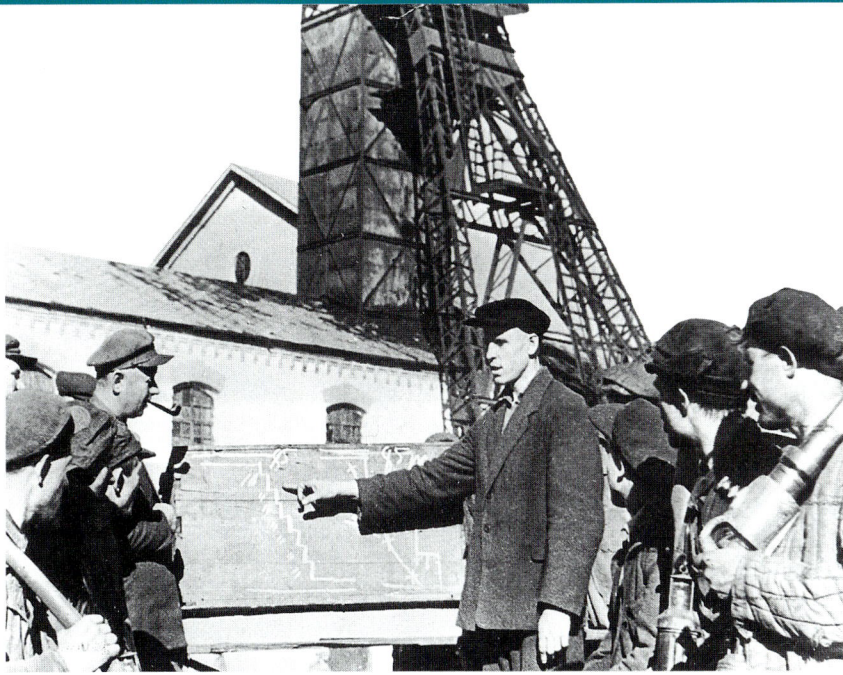

SOURCE 18
Alexei Stakhanov.

Think about...

1 Why did agriculture and industry have to be changed?

2 Which policy was more successful – collectivisation of agriculture or the Five-Year Plans for industry?

3 Did the people benefit from these policies either in the short term or the long term?

Persuasion and toughness

The main problem facing Stalin and Soviet economic planners in the 1930s was how to get high levels of effort from workers who were poorly paid and often new to factory work. Large numbers of workers in Russian factories in the 1930s had begun their working lives as peasants. They were used to working extremely hard at some points in the year – such as harvest time – and taking it slightly easier at others. This attitude was transferred to industry, where it was not at all appropriate.

Stalin's solution was a mixture of persuasion and toughness. Propaganda campaigns were mounted to encourage people to work harder. Films, books and newspapers glorified effort. One of the best-known campaigns featured a Ukrainian miner, Alexei Stakhanov (Source 18), who in 1934 in one six-hour shift allegedly cut 102 tons of coal when his target was a mere 7 tons. Workers were encouraged to do as well or better than Stakhanov. In effect, the 'Stakhanovite movement', as it became known, was an attempt to pressurise workers into competing against each other: though in Soviet propaganda the phrase 'socialist emulation' was used rather than 'competition'. This was because competition was something which occurred in the capitalist world and was therefore a dirty word in Stalin's Russia. How successful was the Soviet propaganda campaign? Many workers were no doubt persuaded to work harder, but not everyone was swayed by Soviet industrialisation propaganda (see Source 19).

Toughness came in the form of harsh punishments. In 1932 absenteeism was defined as one day of absence from work without good reason: in 1939 it was 20 minutes late without good reason. A worker guilty of absenteeism lost his or her job and the ration card and the flat that went with it. In 1940 absenteeism became a criminal offence punishable by six months' hard labour.

Another way in which workers were intimidated was through the prosecution of alleged SABOTEURS. The earliest example of this was the so-called 'Shakhty trial' (1928), in which 53 engineers were accused of wrecking industrial equipment. Five of the accused were executed. Another prosecution of this kind was the 'Metrovick' trial (1933) in which Britons working in Russia were among the accused. The message was clear: anyone obstructing the industrialisation drive would be shown no mercy.

SOURCE 19

People are sick of Stakhanov, quite apart from whether they approve – as some do – or disapprove of the movement. People are sick and tired of listening to speeches. They cut off the wireless. They are likewise tired of contemplating the monstrous portraits of Soviet heroes.

(British consul in Leningrad, 1936.)

Review

Look back over pages 34 to 37. Stalin was determined to modernise Soviet Russia. See especially Source 9 on page 34.

The great terror: Stalin's purges 1936 to 1939

In December 1934 Sergei Kirov, the young and popular Communist Party chief in Leningrad, was murdered. It is now thought likely that the murder took place on Stalin's orders. At the time, however, the blame was put on 14 men who had links with Kamenev and Zinoviev: they were swiftly executed after a secret trial.

1936 saw the first of a series of 'show trials' in which leading communists – no doubt after torture and threats to their families – publicly confessed to outrageous crimes and were sentenced to death (see Sources 20, 21 and 22). The confessions were extracted by the security force known as the Cheka but renamed the NKVD in 1934 (the letters stand for the Commissariat for Internal Affairs). In the years of the 'great terror' the NKVD was headed in turn by Genrikh Yagoda (1934 to 1936), Nikolai Yezhov (1936 to 1938) and Lavrenti Beria (1938 to 1953). The 'show trials' were stage-managed on Stalin's orders by Andrei Vyshinsky, chief state prosecutor and a former Menshevik.

The victims

The 'great terror' saw the death or imprisonment of millions of Soviet citizens, as Source 23 shows. The high command of the Red Army was hit particularly hard. So were the 'Old Bolsheviks' – people who had

▲ SOURCE 20
Andrei Vyshinsky summing up at the 'show trials'.

▼ SOURCE 21
An American cartoonist's view of the 'show trials'.

SOURCE 22 ►
The purges.

Time chart

Date	Principal defendants	Crimes of which defendants were accused
1936	Kamenev	• Murder of Kirov • Plotting to murder Stalin
	Zinoviev	• Organising a 'terrorist centre' for Trotsky
1937	Radek	• Plotting with Trotsky
1938	Bukharin	• Spying for Japan and Germany
	Yagoda (former secret police chief)	• Plotting with Trotsky • Spying for Japan and Germany • Plotting to murder Lenin in 1918

been members of the Bolshevik Party before the October Revolution. Science, technology and the arts also fared badly: among the most distinguished victims of the purges were Lev Landau (physicist), Nikolai Vavilov (biologist), A.N. Tupolev (aircraft designer), Isaac Babel (novelist) and Osip Mandelshtam (poet). No one, however, was safe.

Millions of ordinary people were arrested after neighbours or workmates informed the NKVD that they were 'enemies of the people'. As many as one in five of the Soviet Union's urban population were what were known as 'seksots' – NKVD informers. Often 'seksots' gave people's names to the authorities in order to settle old private scores or for some other reason which had nothing to do with politics.

Victims of the PURGES who escaped execution were sent to NKVD labour camps. Most of these were located in the remote Arctic and eastern regions of the Soviet Union. They were run by a department of the NKVD called the GULAG. Only the very strongest survived the camps: prisoners had to do 12 or more hours of physical labour each day, often in very low temperatures, on meagre rations.

Why did the purges take place?

Stalin's purges are not only horrifying but baffling, too. They did the Soviet Union untold harm. Industry lost many of its best managers and technical experts. The army lost its most experienced commanders at a time of growing international tension. Source 24 gives Stalin's own explanation of why the purges took place. Sources 25 and 26 are explanations of the purges which have been offered by historians.

SOURCE 23 Victims of the purges, 1937–1938	
Executed	1 million
Died in camps	2 million
In prison, late 1938	1 million
In labour camps, late 1938	8 million

SOURCE 24

Among the Trotskyites and Zinovievites fascism found faithful servants who were ready to work for the defeat of the Soviet Union in order to restore capitalism. Trotsky, Zinoviev and Kamenev had been in conspiracy against Lenin, the Party and the Soviet state ever since the October Revolution.

(From Stalin's *History of the Communist Party of the Soviet Union*, 1939.)

SOURCE 25

I cannot resist the conclusion that from his middle fifties Stalin was the subject of persecution mania to an extent which went a long way beyond reason.

(C.P. Snow, British writer and politician, 1967.)

SOURCE 26

The purge reduced Stalin's ever-present fear of conspiracy, overthrow and assassination. It silenced opposition for good and cleared the way to an autocratic form of rule.

(Alan Bullock, British historian, 1991.)

Assessment

1 In what ways does Source 24 give a distorted view of history?

2 To what extent is the interpretation of Stalin's purges given in Source 26 supported by the evidence of Sources 20 to 23?

3 Suggest reasons why Source 24 explains the purges in the way it does.

4 The truth about the purges was not published in the USSR until long after Stalin's death. What does this tell us about Soviet society in those decades?

5 'A completely satisfactory explanation of the reasons for Stalin's purges will never be written.' Would you agree with this view? Give reasons for your answer.

Russia at war: the German threat

Hitler's rise to power in Germany in 1933 was an alarming development from the Soviet point of view. Hitler despised Communism and talked openly of seizing land from Soviet Russia (see Source 27). He called Russians 'Untermenschen', or sub-human.

From the mid-1930s Soviet Russia was ready to collaborate with other countries which had reason to fear Hitler, notably Britain and France. At this time, however, Britain and France were committed to a policy which involved making agreements with Hitler – the 1938 Munich agreement, for example – rather than standing up to him. When Britain abandoned this appeasement policy in 1939 and opened talks with Russia about an anti-Hitler alliance, Stalin was deeply suspicious. He believed Britain wanted to stand on the sidelines while Nazi Germany and Soviet Russia tore each other to pieces.

The Non-Aggression Pact

The Anglo-Russian alliance talks came to nothing. Instead, to the astonishment of the outside world, Russia made an agreement with Germany – the 1939 Nazi-Soviet Non-Aggression Pact – under which the two countries pledged not to go to war against each other. They also agreed to divide Poland between them. In this way, Soviet Russia regained the land that it had surrendered to Poland under the Treaty of Riga in 1921.

For Hitler the Non-Aggression Pact was simply a way of ensuring that he did not have to contend with Russia when he attacked Poland. Hitler never intended to stick to the agreement. It is possible, however, that Stalin believed that he would.

"COME ON, JOE, THOSE TROUSERS WILL FIT ME FINE . . ."

▲ **SOURCE 27**
Hitler's aims as seen by the *Daily Herald*, a British newspaper, in July 1941.

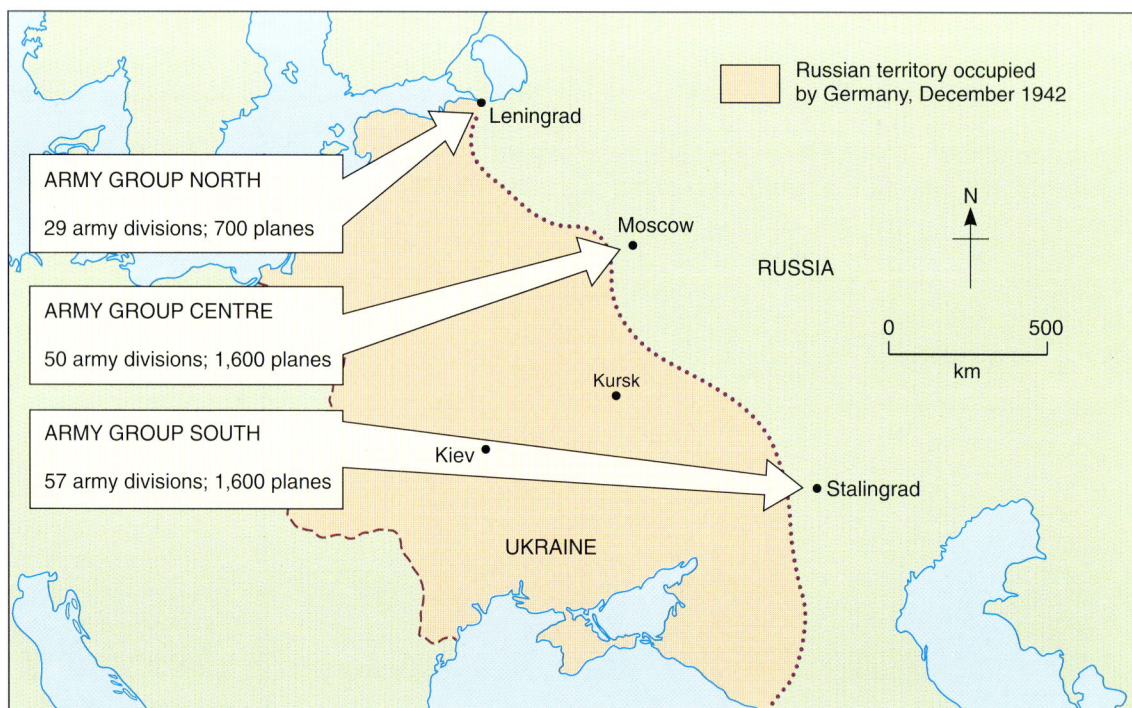

SOURCE 28 ▶
'Operation Barbarossa' – the German attack on Russia, 1941. The German invasion was made up of 3.2 million men, 3,350 tanks and 3,000 aircraft.

Russian territory occupied by Germany, December 1942

ARMY GROUP NORTH
29 army divisions; 700 planes

ARMY GROUP CENTRE
50 army divisions; 1,600 planes

ARMY GROUP SOUTH
57 army divisions; 1,600 planes

Leningrad

Moscow

RUSSIA

Kursk

Kiev

Stalingrad

UKRAINE

N

0   500
km

Germany declares war

On 22 June 1941, without warning, Germany declared war on Russia. Stalin had been told by his spies and by foreign agents that Hitler was planning an invasion, but he refused to believe them. Russia's front-line defences were quickly overrun. In the first four months of fighting, the Germans destroyed 20,000 Soviet tanks and took two million Russians prisoner.

The German attack was three-pronged (see Source 28). Germany's Army Group North struck at Leningrad. Between 1941 and early 1944 Leningrad and its three million citizens were under siege. They were supplied by the 'Lifeline Road' which included carrying supplies across the ice of Lake Ladoga (see Source 29). Despite the heroic efforts of the townspeople, one million Leningraders died during the 890 days of the siege.

Army Group Centre's target was Moscow. By October 1941 German troops were within sight of the Russian capital. They were beaten off by a counter-attack led by Marshal Zhukov. Another factor which helped to save Moscow was a Russian winter of exceptional severity. The invaders were not equipped to deal with very low temperatures.

The German Army Group South invaded the Ukraine. In September 1941 it took Kiev, the Ukraine's capital, and then pushed on in the direction of the Baku oilfield.

The battles of Stalingrad and Kursk

It was in southern Russia that two of the most important battles of the Second World War took place. One was at Stalingrad, where for five months (September 1942 to January 1943) German and Russian infantrymen fought street by street for control of the city (see Source 30). Eventually, the Germans were forced to surrender. The second great battle took place at Kursk in July 1943. Incensed by the defeat at Stalingrad, Hitler ordered his ARMOURED DIVISIONS on to the attack. They were broken by the Red Army in the greatest tank battle the world has seen (Source 31).

After Kursk, the Germans were remorselessly forced back. By mid-1944, Soviet Russia had cleared its own territory of German troops. In early 1945, the Red Army entered Germany.

▲ **SOURCE 29**
Lorry crossing Lake Ladoga, Winter, 1941.

SOURCE 30 ►
Fighting during the battle of Stalingrad, 1942 to 1943.

▼ **SOURCE 31**
Russian stamp showing the battle of Kursk, July 1943.

QUESTIONS

1 *What does Source 27 suggest were Hitler's motives for attacking Russia?*

2 *How might Source 28 be used to offer support for the view of Hitler's motives for attacking Russia suggested in Source 27?*

3 *Making use of Sources 30 and 31, show how the battles of Stalingrad and Kursk differed in character.*

Why did Russia defeat Germany in the War?

The first reaction of the Russian people to the German invasion of 1941 was not always one of fierce hostility. In some places, notably the Ukraine, the Germans were welcomed as liberators. Among the Red Army soldiers who were taken prisoner in 1941 was some willingness to change sides and fight alongside the Germans: General Andrei Vlasov became the leader of these RENEGADES.

The uncertain mood of 1941 soon changed, however. A hatred of Germany emerged as well as a determination to win the war. Sources 32, 33 and 34 help to explain why this change came about.

▲ **SOURCE 32**
German treatment of Russian civilian resistance fighters, 1941.

SOURCE 33

After a long battle for Davydovo, a village in the Moscow region, our company was given permission to clean up. We started looking for a well. The well was full of the corpses of children, from tiny infants to some about five years old.

(A Russian soldier remembers 1941.)

SOURCE 34

Every piece of territory which has to be abandoned to the enemy must be rendered unusable as far as possible. Every settlement must be burnt down and destroyed without consideration for the population.

(Hitler, speaking after the battle for Moscow in 1941.)

Stalin's leadership

The will to fight shown by the Russian people in 1941 to 1945 was not simply the result of enemy atrocities. Stalin's leadership was also a factor. During the war years, the character of Stalin's rule changed. It became less harsh and oppressive. There was some relaxation of censorship. Because leaders of the Orthodox Church gave strong support to the war effort, restrictions on the churches were eased: thousands of churches which had been closed were allowed to re-open. In the countryside, the peasantry and collective farms were now less tightly supervised than they had been during the 1930s – many peasants took the opportunity to extend their private plots at the expense of the kolkhozy. Propaganda changed, too.

Wartime propaganda

In the war years, Communist slogans disappeared from Soviet propaganda. Wartime propaganda featured heroes of Russia's Tsarist past such as Peter the Great and Marshal Kutuzov (see Source 35). Before the war, it had always been suggested that there was nothing good about the Tsarist era in Russian history. The reason for the change is obvious: Stalin wanted to appeal to the patriotism of the Russian people. This emphasis on arousing people's sense of patriotism is also evident in the names used to describe the war: the 'Great Patriotic War' or the 'Great Fatherland War'. There was also a new acknowledgement in wartime propaganda of the efforts of Russia's allies, Britain and the United States (see Source 36). In the 1930s, official propaganda had often ridiculed foreigners.

SOURCE 35
'May Our Great Forefathers Inspire Us!' – Soviet poster, 1941. The figure shown is Marshal Kutuzov who defeated Napoleon at the battle of Borodino in 1812 when he tried to invade Russia.

SOURCE 36
'From this noose he will never escape' – Soviet poster, 1942.

Why was Soviet Russia successful?

The determination shown by its people was one of the main reasons why Soviet Russia was eventually able to defeat Hitler's armies. Here are the other principal reasons for Soviet Russia's success:

- The Soviet generals, Marshal Zhukov in particular, were skilful and ruthless. Zhukov did not shrink from buying success by accepting heavy losses among his troops.

- Soviet weaponry was of high quality. The T34 tank, the Katyusha rocket launcher and the Sturmovik ground attack aircraft were as good as anything the Germans had.

- Hitler made some serious mistakes. In 1941 his armies were not properly equipped for winter warfare. In early 1942 he refused to cut his losses by allowing a retreat from Stalingrad. The attack he ordered at Kursk a few months later was predictable and ill-judged.

- Soviet Russia received extensive aid from its allies, Britain and the United States. This came in two forms: massive arms shipments and information about German plans obtained by British code-breakers.

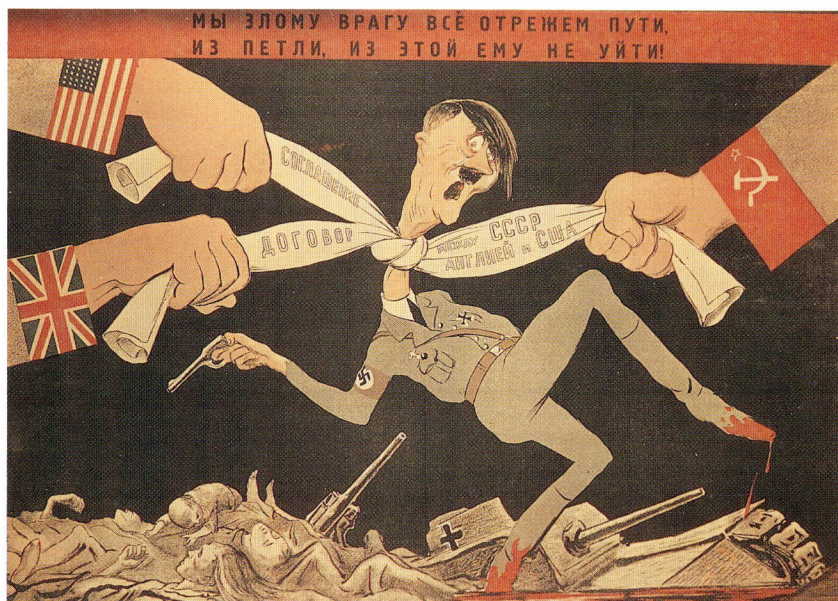

Assessment

1 *Suggest reasons why the German army was welcomed in some parts of Russia.*

2 *How did German treatment of the areas and people they conquered turn people against them?*

3 *Several reasons for Russian success in the Second World War are given here. Choose three and explain them. Which of the three you have chosen do you think was the most important?*

4 *What links are there between the three reasons you have chosen?*

Cost of the war

The cost of the war to the Soviet Union was immense. Between 1941 and 1945, 20 million Russians died. This was more than a tenth of the total Russian population. In 1945, millions more were homeless. Up to 70,000 villages and 1,700 towns and cities were classified as destroyed. The country's industrial base was broken and disorganised. Thousands of factories had been wrecked; others had been moved eastwards as the Germans approached. The condition of agriculture was just as bad: tens of thousands of collective farms lay in ruins.

Stalin's last years: 1945 to 1953

The Russian people may have thought in 1945 that Stalin would reward them for their efforts in the 'Great Patriotic War' by allowing them more freedom and by trying to raise living standards. If so, they were mistaken.

Stalin's priority in 1945 was the restoration of Soviet heavy industry. The process was begun with the Fourth Five-Year Plan (1946 to 1950). Once again, Russians were called upon to work very hard and to endure great hardship (see Source 37).

In the countryside, Stalin clamped down hard on the peasantry. Agriculture was re-collectivised after the wartime breakdown. A decree was issued in 1946 forcing peasants to hand back to the collective farms any land taken during the war.

When peace came, strict censorship was re-imposed. Contacts between Russians and foreigners, which during the war had been quite extensive, ended. Soviet Russia became a closed society. West European and American culture was fiercely attacked (see Source 38 for an example).

After the defeat of Germany, the Stalin 'personality cult' reached new heights. At Communist Party gatherings Stalin was met with such greetings as 'Shining sun of humanity', 'Creator of all our victories' and 'Greatest genius in history'. No one else was allowed to share the limelight. Marshal Zhukov, victor of the battles of Moscow and Stalingrad, was relieved of his command and disappeared from public view.

T. D. Lysenko

One man who basked in Stalin's favour in the late 1940s was the biologist T. D. Lysenko. Lysenko denied that genes were responsible for the characteristics inherited by plants and animals. He claimed instead that characteristics could be inherited from the environment. Lysenko's ideas were proclaimed by the Communists to be 'socialist' and right: conventional GENETICS were condemned as 'bourgeois' and wrong. Lysenko's theories lay behind Stalin's 'Plan for the Transformation of Nature' in 1949 – an enormous tree-planting scheme which, it was claimed, would change the climate of southern Russia. It failed.

Investigation

Was Stalin's rule between 1945 and his death in 1953 more or less oppressive than it had been in the 1930s?

▲ **SOURCE 37**
'Fulfil the Five-Year Plan in Four Years' – a Soviet poster, 1948.

> ## SOURCE 38
>
> West European and American culture is putrid in its moral foundations. The entire host of writers, film-makers and theatrical producers strives to shift the attention of the advanced elements in society from political and social questions into the channel of vulgar and empty art, crowded with gangsters, chorus girls, praise of adultery, and the affairs of adventurers and rogues of every kind.
>
> (Andrei Zhdanov, Communist boss in Leningrad, the Communist Party's cultural expert and Politburo member, 1946.)

Return of the purges

The late 1940s saw the return of purges. The sudden death in 1948 of Andrei Zhdanov was followed by the 'Leningrad Affair', a purge of the city's Communist Party. At the time of Stalin's death, a more extensive purge seemed to be in the offing. In January 1953, it was announced that nine KREMLIN doctors had confessed to the murder of Zhdanov. The announcement of the 'Doctors' Plot' was followed by a hunt for more 'traitors'. In the next few months, 8,000 people were arrested.

SOURCE 39 ►
Soviet satellite states
in Eastern Europe, in
the late 1940s.

FINLAND

Lake Ladoga

SWEDEN

Leningrad

DENMARK

ESTONIA

LATVIA

LITHUANIA

Soviet gains
1939-1940

Soviet gains
after 1945

Berlin

1949 E.
GERMANY

1947
POLAND

N

W. GERMANY

1948
CZECHOSLOVAKIA

0   500
km

AUSTRIA

1947
HUNGARY

1948
ROMANIA

ITALY

YUGOSLAVIA

1948
BULGARIA

Expansion in Eastern Europe

If one of the distinguishing features of
Stalin's last years was renewed brutality at
home, another was the Soviet takeover of
Eastern Europe. Between 1945 and 1949,
regimes of a Stalinist kind were established
in each of the states 'liberated' by the Red
Army (see Source 39). Soviet Russia co-
ordinated the activities of the Communist
parties in these states through 'Cominform'
(Communist Information Bureau,
established in 1947). It co-ordinated
economic activity in them through
'Comecon' (Council of Mutual Economic
Assistance, founded in 1949).

Soviet expansion in Eastern Europe was
the principal cause of the 'Cold War' – the
conflict between Russia and the free or
capitalist world which broke out after the
defeat of Hitler. The 'COLD WAR' not only
meant continuing tension but also involved
a nuclear ARMS RACE which the Soviet Union
could ill afford. Why then did Stalin expand
into Eastern Europe? Some historians argue
that Soviet policy was nakedly aggressive,
part of an attempt to establish Communist
mastery over the world. Others maintain
that Stalin, conscious of the extent to which
the war had weakened the Soviet Union,
took control of Eastern Europe in order to
create a defensive buffer zone between
Russia and the West. Even Stalin's own
comments on the matter do not solve the
problem (see Sources 40 and 41).

SOURCE 40

We cannot for one minute forget the basic truth that our
country remains the one socialist state in the world. I am
convinced the capitalist states will not rest until they have
destroyed us.

(Stalin, speaking to Bedell Smith, the US ambassador
to the Soviet Union, 1946.)

SOURCE 41

This war is not as in the past:
whoever occupies a territory also
imposes on it his own social
system. Everyone imposes his own
social system as far as his army
has power to do so.

(Stalin, speaking in a private
conversation with Milovan Djilas
and fellow Communists, 1945.)

QUESTIONS

1   'In some ways the quality of life of the
    Soviet people worsened when the war
    ended.' What evidence could be offered in
    support of this claim?

2   What, according to Zhdanov, was the
    proper role of writers and film-makers?
    With your knowledge of 'Socialist
    Realism', do you think that the role
    Zhdanov suggests is the one that Soviet
    artists actually performed in the 1930s
    and 1940s?

3   Study Sources 40 and 41. Are there any
    reasons to believe that Stalin's remarks
    to Djilas give a true indication of his
    motives for occupying Eastern Europe
    while those made to Bedell Smith do not?

Stalin: interpretations

What judgements have people made on Stalin after his death?

Josef Stalin died in 1953 aged 73. Apart from the war years, when he had met the leaders of Britain and the United States at SUMMIT CONFERENCES at Tehran (1943), Yalta (1945) and Potsdam (1945), Stalin lived an isolated life in the Kremlin. Few people encountered him at close quarters. Those who did, found him suspicious and frightening. Stalin's isolation and secretive nature mean that there is a shortage of documentary evidence relating to his key decisions. Why was the New Economic Policy abandoned so suddenly in 1928–1929? Why did the purges continue in the later 1930s? Why was Russia taken by surprise in 1941, given that Soviet intelligence had evidence that a German attack was imminent? Until recently, historians have had only scraps of evidence.

▲ **SOURCE 42**
'It's strange how you remind me of someone, Josef' – cartoon by David Low, 1936.

Suddenly there is almost too much information for them to digest – from the availability of the entire KGB secret files, to the memoirs of people who now have the freedom to write about this time in Soviet history. However, despite this new wealth of evidence, there is very little from Stalin himself.

In the 1930s Stalinist Russia and Nazi Germany were often seen as being at different ends of the political spectrum – Nazi Germany on the far right, Soviet Russia on the far left. What has impressed western historians who have written about the two regimes since 1945 is not their differences but their similarities. Both exhibit strong totalitarian characteristics, such as single-party rule, secret police forces operating outside the law, concentration camps and INDOCTRINATION. The fact that there were basic similarities between Nazism and Stalinism did not escape the notice of everyone in the 1930s (see Source 42).

SOURCE 43

Since 1930 Stalin had enlarged the industrial base. But he had done so by very wasteful methods. He had not made the best use of his resources, wasting much of the original skilled engineering force by decimating it on false charges of sabotage. Even in 1929 it was reasonably clear, economically speaking, that milder measures could have produced equally good results.

(Robert Conquest, British historian, 1968.)

SOURCE 44

Russia could never have become a superpower without a coercive regime. Its manpower was unsuited to industrial discipline, entirely lacking that mysterious quality which makes the Japanese seemingly enjoy the drudgery of production-line labour. When it comes to industrial discipline, Russians are free spirits, incapable of creating their own work ethic. Stalin's labour regulations were essential if his country was to become an industrial superpower.

(Alex de Jonge, British historian, 1986.)

New interpretations?
Was Stalin simply an evil and destructive TYRANT like Hitler? This is not a view all western historians would accept. Some maintain that Stalin's goals, though often pursued by hideous methods, were in themselves worthwhile. This is especially true of Stalin's industrialisation drive. The question can be asked whether industrial growth of the kind which took place in the 1930s could only have been achieved by Stalinist methods (see Sources 43 and 44).

In Russia itself, full and free discussion of the Stalinist years was not possible so long as the Communist Party remained in power. What was said about Stalin in public changed as Soviet leaders came and went. Nikita Khrushchev launched a savage attack in private on aspects of Stalin's rule at the

Twentieth Communist Party Congress in 1956. News of what he said soon leaked out to the people of the Soviet Union and to the world. In the Brezhnev years (1964 to 1982), there was official silence on the subject of Stalin's wrongdoings. Discussion of his crimes by others was stopped. A small statue of him appeared near Lenin's mausoleum, suggesting that he was seen as a leader whose memory should be respected.

There were renewed attacks on Stalin under Mikhail Gorbachev, one of whose policies was 'glasnost', or openness. It is notable, though, that neither Gorbachev nor Khrushchev before him condemned all aspects of Stalin's rule. Source 45 shows what Khrushchev and Gorbachev had to say about key issues of Stalin's rule.

▼ SOURCE 45
Khrushchev and Gorbachev on Stalin.

1 Do you think any of the statements made by Khrushchev or Gorbachev in Source 45 are factually incorrect?

2 Study Sources 43 and 44. Which of these two interpretations do you find the more persuasive – de Jonge's or Conquest's?

3 Can you see any indications in Source 45 of either Khrushchev or Gorbachev trying to justify their own positions and policies in what they say about Stalin? (See unit 4 for their positions and policies.)

Subject	Nikita Khrushchev, 1956	Mikhail Gorbachev, 1987
Trotsky	'The Party fought a serious fight against the Trotskyites and disarmed the enemies of Leninism ... as a result it was strengthened. Here Stalin played a positive role.'	'Trotsky displayed excessive pretensions to top leadership. The Party's leading nucleus, headed by Stalin, safeguarded Leninism in ideological struggle.'
Collectivisation and industrialisation	'Consider what would have happened in 1928–1929 if the policy of the Right Opposition had been followed. We would not now have a powerful heavy industry and we would not have the kolkhozy.'	'The period saw losses. People began to believe in the universal effectiveness of rigid centralisation. Nor were excesses avoided in the struggle against the kulaks. The basically correct policy of fighting the kulaks was often interpreted so broadly that it swept in a considerable part of the middle peasantry. All this had a dire effect on the country's socio-political development.'
The Purges	'Many thousands of honest and innocent Communists have died as a result of monstrous falsification. Stalin used terroristic methods against honest Soviet people.'	'The guilt of Stalin for the wholesale repressive measures and acts of lawlessness is enormous and unforgivable. Accusations against many Communists and non-Party people were a result of deliberate falsification.'
Second World War	'The necessary steps were not taken to prevent the country from being caught unawares. Even after the war began, the nervousness and hysteria which Stalin demonstrated caused our army serious damage.'	'A factor in the achievement of victory was the tremendous will, purposefulness and persistence, ability to organise and discipline people displayed in the war years by Stalin.'

Khrushchev
Retreat

Nikita Khrushchev emerged as Stalin's successor after a brief power struggle. He was the USSR's leader for ten years. In this unit we will find out about the ways in which he tackled the problems at home and abroad he inherited from Stalin. Under Khrushchev some things changed, but many others stayed the same.

Mikhail Gorbachev became the USSR's leader in 1985. Gorbachev tried to make fundamental changes – far more fundamental than anything attempted by Khrushchev – but in the process he unleashed forces that shook the Soviet Union to pieces. We will find out about these changes and see how Communist rule collapsed in Russia.

▲ **SOURCE 1**
Khrushchev at the United Nations, 1960.

Key Questions

How effective were Khrushchev's reforms?

Was Khrushchev a liberal?

Did the Cuban missile crisis cause Khrushchev's downfall?

How fundamental were Gorbachev's reforms?

Why did the Soviet Union disintegrate in 1991?

In 1953 Khrushchev (Source 1) was Communist Party boss in Moscow and one of the Party's experts on agricultural matters. He had been born into a peasant household near Kursk in 1894. He joined the Bolsheviks during the Civil War, and subsequently – thanks in part to the sponsorship of one of Stalin's main henchmen, Lazar Kaganovich – he rose through the ranks of the Communist Party.

During his time as Soviet leader, Khrushchev never had the kind of control over the Communist Party enjoyed by Lenin and Stalin. Khrushchev did not have prestige comparable to Lenin's and people were not terrified of him as they were of Stalin.

In manner and style Khrushchev differed greatly from Stalin. He was not a remote figure who hid himself from public view. He was outgoing and relished foreign travel (see Source 2). Nor did he keep his emotions tightly under control in the way that Stalin had done: he was impulsive and hot-tempered. Politically this was a weakness. Incidents such as the one at the United Nations General Assembly in 1960 where he interrupted another speaker by banging his shoe on his desk, or his crude public outburst

from Stalinism

Source 2 Khrushchev's main foreign visits, 1953 to 1964

China	1954, 1958, 1959
Yugoslavia	1955
Summit Conference, Geneva	1955
India	1955, 1960
United Kingdom	1956
Poland	1956
Germany	1959
United States	1959
France	1960
Summit Conference, Paris	1960
UN General Assembly, New York	1960
Egypt	1964

▼ SOURCE 4
German cartoon, 1956, showing Khrushchev (with halo) heaping the bodies of purge victims on to Stalin's head.

SOURCE 3

Khrushchev began his inspection in the room where paintings by Bilyutin and other friends of mine had been hung. He swore horribly and became extremely angry about them. It was there he said 'a donkey could do better with his tail'. Khrushchev said I devoured the people's money and produced manure.

(Ernst Neivestny, sculptor, recalling Khrushchev's visit to a modern art exhibition, 1962.)

against modern art in 1962, allowed his enemies to claim that he lacked proper dignity (see Source 3).

Style of leadership

Khrushchev differed from Stalin in his style of leadership. Were there more important differences too? Khrushchev certainly got rid of the visible signs of the Stalin 'personality cult'. Statues and posters of Stalin were taken down. Towns named after Stalin were renamed (for instance, Stalingrad became Volgograd). One interpretation of all this was that Khrushchev was a reformer and a liberal. Others suggested that he was trying to off-load the blame for crimes which he and others could have done more to prevent (see Source 4).

Khrushchev was overthrown in 1964, two years after the Cuban missile crisis. He was the first Soviet leader to live in retirement. Both of his predecessors had died in office. One thing at least had changed since Stalin's day: the penalty for political defeat was no longer death.

Mikhail Gorbachev

Under Khrushchev the Soviet system of economic planning had started to creak badly. By 1985, when Gorbachev came to power, things were much worse. Productivity in both industry and agriculture was far below Western standards. The same was true of living standards. One Soviet joke about the economic system ran 'We pretend to work, and they pretend to pay us.' Gorbachev was determined to build a more dynamic and prosperous economy. This meant a move away from rigid central planning. Gorbachev could not have guessed that within six years the Soviet Union would no longer exist.

▲ SOURCE 5
Mourners at Stalin's tomb, 1953 (left to right): Khrushchev, Beria, Malenkov, Bulganin, Voroshilov, Kaganovich.

Khrushchev: superpower leader

Power struggle, 1953 to 1957

In 1953 a number of rivals stood between Nikita Khrushchev and the leadership of Soviet Russia (see Source 5). There was Lavrenti Beria, chief of the secret police. There were the hard-line Stalinists, Vyacheslav Molotov and Lazar Kaganovich. Hard-line Stalinists supported the fixed set of ideas laid down by Stalin and refused to accept any change in them. Khrushchev's most formidable rival, though, was not a hard-line Stalinist but a would-be reformer, Georgy Malenkov. In 1953 Malenkov became Soviet prime minister.

Beria was quickly removed from the scene. All of the other leading Communists who were jockeying for position in 1953 distrusted Beria and feared the secret police empire he headed. In July 1953 Beria was arrested and executed. Khrushchev was the main organiser of Beria's downfall.

Khrushchev then plotted against Malenkov. In 1953 Malenkov had called for a change of direction in Soviet economic policy. Under this so-called 'New Course', greater emphasis was to be placed on the production of food and consumer goods and less on heavy industry. These proposals were not acceptable to the hard-line Stalinists. They wanted the emphasis to remain on heavy industry (as a result they were described as 'metal eaters'). Khrushchev acted as their spokesman. In 1955 Malenkov was forced to resign as prime minister. Khrushchev was now the dominant figure in Soviet politics. He then proceeded to outrage the 'metal eaters' by adopting Malenkov's ideas.

In 1957 the hard-line Stalinists, supported by Malenkov, made a determined bid to overthrow Khrushchev. The Communist Party's PRAESIDIUM voted seven to four to remove him from office. Khrushchev appealed to the Party's Central Committee and was able to get this decision reversed. The penalty which the 'Anti-Party Group', as Khrushchev labelled them, paid for defeat was disgrace – not, as would have happened in Stalin's day, execution. Molotov became Soviet ambassador to Mongolia, Kaganovich became a cement factory manager in Siberia and Malenkov became a power station manager in Soviet Asia.

Khrushchev's victory in 1957 did not make him an unchallenged dictator as Stalin had been. Throughout the remaining years of his leadership he had to be mindful of opinion within the Communist Party. Sometimes he had to change his policies because he could not carry the Party with him. In the end he lost his Party's confidence.

The Soviet superpower

The international position of Khrushchev's Russia was very different from that of Stalin's Russia in the 1930s. Stalin's Russia had been one among half a dozen or so great powers which were roughly comparable in terms of military strength. Khrushchev's Russia was one of two superpowers, the other being the United States of America. These two superpowers dwarfed other states in terms of their military strength, based on their nuclear weapons (see the fact file opposite), their economic resources and the extent of their influence. Under Stalin in the 1930s, Soviet Russia's ambitions had not, in practice, extended far beyond its own borders. Under

The Soviet–United States arms race in the Khrushchev era

The Soviet Union exploded its first atomic bomb in 1949, four years after the United States.

In 1954, one year after the United States, Soviet Russia exploded its first hydrogen (or thermonuclear) bomb. The hydrogen bomb, much more powerful than the atomic bomb, releases vast amounts of energy.

In Khrushchev's time there was not only competition between Soviet Russia and the United States to build more powerful bombs, but also to improve delivery systems – the means of getting bombs to their targets.

The delivery systems in use in the mid-1950s were long-range manned bombers, like the Soviet 'Bison' and 'Bear' and the American B-52. Bombers, however, could be shot down.

The next step was inter-continental ballistic missiles (ICBMs), such as the Soviet SS-11 and the American 'Titan' which were launched from underground bases (or 'silos').

In theory, ICBM 'silos' could be detected and attacked. The two superpowers therefore developed submarine launched ballistic missiles (SLBMs): the Soviet SS-N5 and the American 'Polaris'. The submarines from which these missiles were launched could roam the oceans and were virtually undetectable. SLBMs were coming into service as Khrushchev left office.

▼ SOURCE 6
Living standards compared: ownership of consumer goods in the USA and Soviet Russia in the mid-1960s (number per 1,000 of population).

Khrushchev it became a world power, with – among other things – an immensely powerful navy. This was built up after 1957 under the direction of Admiral Gorshkov.

In the 1950s the Soviet Union matched the United States in military strength, and in some aspects of science and technology it appeared to forge ahead. In 1957 Soviet Russia put the first satellite (the 'Sputnik') into orbit, and four years later Yuri Gagarin became the first man in space. Soviet living standards, however, as Source 6 shows, lagged a long way behind those of the United States. This was something Khrushchev boasted would be reversed sooner rather than later (Source 7).

SOURCE 7

In the current decade (1961 to 1970) the Soviet Union will surpass the strongest and richest capitalist country, the United States, in production per head of the population; the people's standard of living will improve substantially; everyone will live in easy circumstances.

(Khrushchev, addressing the 22nd Communist Party Congress, 1961.)

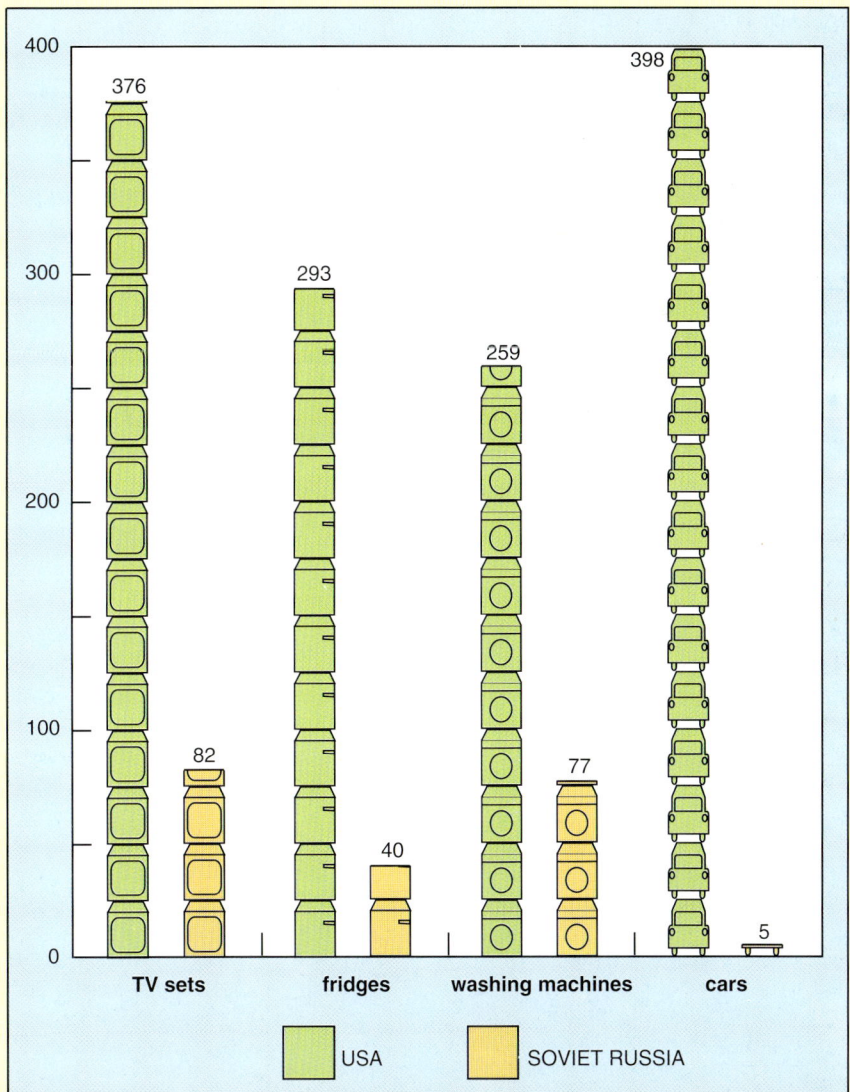

	TV sets	fridges	washing machines	cars
USA	376	293	259	398
SOVIET RUSSIA	82	40	77	5

How much did life in Russia change under Khrushchev?

Khrushchev's domestic policies involved both change and continuity. Some of the worst features of Stalinist rule were removed, but the basis on which the Soviet economy operated was left largely unaltered. It would have been surprising had it been otherwise. Khrushchev's famous 'secret speech' to the Twentieth Party Congress in 1956 condemned Stalin's personality cult and aspects of the 'great terror' but contained no criticism of collectivisation or of the industrialisation drive of the 1930s.

'Socialist legality'

Under Khrushchev, the GULAG labour camps were officially abolished. Millions of 'zeks' – labour camp detainees – were released. A new Criminal Code, introduced in 1958, laid down the principle that no one could be imprisoned except by a proper court of law. The power of the secret police – renamed the KGB in 1954 – was thus, in theory, sharply reduced. Khrushchev spoke of a return to the principle of 'socialist legality' (Source 8). It was true that in the Khrushchev era the Soviet people were not terrorised as they had been under Stalin, but political prisoners did not become a thing of the past (see Source 9). There were ways round the Criminal Code. Under Leonid Brezhnev, Khrushchev's successor, political DISSIDENTS were declared to be suffering from mental illness and were detained in asylums.

Individual freedom

The lives of Soviet people were more secure under Khrushchev than they had been under Stalin. But was there greater freedom? There was certainly some relaxation in censorship. In 1962, for example, Khrushchev allowed the publication of *One Day in the Life of Ivan Denisovich* – Alexander Solzhenitsyn's story about life in a GULAG camp. In general, though, improvements were limited. In religion, Khrushchev was more hostile to the churches than Stalin had been: thousands of Orthodox churches were closed down in an anti-religion drive in the early 1960s. Note, too, that Soviet citizens who displayed open hostility to Communist rule were shown little mercy. In 1962 in the industrial town of Novocherkassk, workers took to the streets in protest against wage cuts and price rises. Among their slogans was 'Use Khrushchev for sausage meat'. Troops opened fire on the crowd, killing at least 80 of the protesters.

SOURCE 8

Now everyone in our country can breathe freely...with no need to worry about the present or the future.

(Khrushchev, speaking in 1963.)

SOURCE 9

There were quite a few people who were not affected by the epidemic of releases under Khrushchev. We have long ago forgotten them in our new lives but they still shuffle hopelessly about the same little patches of trampled earth, with the same watchtowers and barbed wire fences around them. Still, there is really no comparison between the numbers of political prisoners now and in Stalin's time: they are no longer counted in millions or in hundreds of thousands.

(Alexander Solzhenitsyn, former GULAG detainee, writing about the Khrushchev years in 1973.)

The 'Virgin Lands' scheme

Aim
To increase grain production by one third by bringing into use previously uncultivated land in the remoter parts of central and southern Russia (western Siberia and Kazakhstan).

Methods
Half a million volunteers, mostly young, working on newly created state (not collective) farms. On state farms, workers were guaranteed a wage.

Results
Initial success: the grain harvest increased from 83.3 million tonnes in 1953 to 136 million tonnes in 1958, with the 'Virgin Lands' providing over one third of the 1958 total.

Serious setbacks in the early 1960s: over-intensive cultivation and inadequate fertilisation led to serious soil erosion; nearly half of the 'Virgin Lands' area was either ruined or damaged by soil erosion. Harvests in the early 1960s were poor, especially the 1963 harvest.

Industry

Industrial policy under Khrushchev saw some shift in emphasis away from traditional heavy industries – coal and steel – in favour of light engineering, chemical and consumer goods industries. Khrushchev's main industrial reform was the introduction in 1958 of regional economic councils, or sovnarkhozy. The powers of the ministries responsible for industry based in Moscow were transferred to 105 sovnarkhozy. Each sovnarkhoz was to manage the affairs of its own area. On the face of things, the sovnarkhozy were a big step away from the kind of rigid central control Stalin had practised. Appearances, however, were deceptive. The sovnarkhozy were created largely for political reasons. They were a way of taking power away from Khrushchev's opponents – the 'metal eaters' working in the industrial ministries – and putting it into the hands of his supporters. The sovnarkhozy were abandoned after Khrushchev's downfall.

Agriculture

As Soviet leader, Khrushchev was faced with the difficult problem of feeding a growing population with an agricultural system built around state and collective farms. It was a problem he was confident he could solve: Khrushchev thought of himself as an agricultural expert. His solution to the problem was the 'Virgin Lands' scheme, launched in 1954 (see the fact file opposite and Source 10). Khrushchev continued to boast of the scheme's success even after it had run into trouble, as Source 11 shows. Others within Soviet Russia saw the scheme as a disaster which reflected very badly on its originator (see Source 12).

▲ SOURCE10
Combine harvesters at work in the 'Virgin Lands'.

SOURCE 11

If I were in your place I wouldn't divide up the land and portion it out to individual peasants. I would instead set up state farms. We are proceeding with huge land development programmes on the barren STEPPES. Naturally this requires enormous investment but our experience has shown us that three or four good harvests are enough to recoup investment in a state farm. I guarantee a state farm system will make a mint of money for you.

(Khrushchev, speaking to Nasser, the leader of Egypt, 1964.)

SOURCE 12

Politically Khrushchev is suffering a major defeat. Even quite recently he was imprudent enough to poke fun at those who had forecast soil erosion in Kazakhstan; and all these years he has walked in the glory of his success on the agricultural front. His prestige at home is shattered.

(Isaac Deutscher, British historian and commentator on Soviet affairs, writing in 1963.)

Assessment

1   How substantial were the differences between the economic policies of Khrushchev and those of Stalin?

2   Did the people of the Soviet Union find that their lives changed under Khrushchev?

3   Were these changes for the better?

4   Which groups of people found their lives changed a great deal by Khrushchev's policies?

5   'Reform – but only of a very limited kind.' How fair is this comment on the police and prison systems under Khrushchev?

Khrushchev's foreign policy and downfall

Stalin's death in 1953 aroused hopes not only of relaxation inside Russia but also of a lessening of East-West tension. At first it seemed that these hopes might be fulfilled. In 1955 two events took place which promised well for the future: the summit conference between Khrushchev and the United States' President Eisenhower at Geneva and the Austrian State Treaty, under which Soviet Russia and the Western Powers agreed to withdraw their forces from occupied Austria. Then came Hungary.

Following Khrushchev's 'secret speech' of 1956 it was widely believed in Eastern Europe that Soviet Russia was ready to allow its satellite states to regain their independence. Khrushchev, as Source 13 suggests, was faced with a crisis. In Poland rioters demanded freedom from Soviet control. Order was only restored when Wladyslaw Gomulka – a Polish Communist disliked by the Russians but just about acceptable to them – became leader. In Hungary, too, disorder led to the emergence of a new Communist leader, Imre Nagy. Swept along by a tide of popular feeling, Nagy declared himself to be in favour of free elections, the legalisation of political parties other than the Communists and departure from the Warsaw Pact – the 'treaty of friendship, co-operation and mutual aid' signed by Russia and the satellite states in 1955. These things Khrushchev would not tolerate. The Red Army moved into Hungary, crushing the resistance offered both by civilians and by units of the Hungarian army (Source 14). Twenty thousand Hungarians were killed. Nagy was arrested and executed. Soviet control over Eastern Europe was re-established, but the cost to Khrushchev's reputation was considerable.

▼ SOURCE 13
Khrushchev and the performing bears of Eastern Europe, some of them reluctant to do as they are told – a British cartoon, 1956.

▼ SOURCE 14
Russian tanks in Budapest, Hungary, in 1956.

How did Khrushchev behave towards the USA?

How did he treat Soviet satellite states in Eastern Europe?

Why did he fall from power?

World opinion was shocked and dismayed by the brutality of his actions.

Germany, Cuba and the split with China
After the Hungarian uprising, Khrushchev's foreign policy was erratic, BELLIGERENT and unsuccessful.

In 1945 the four Allies split a defeated Germany into four zones of occupation. Special arrangements were made for Berlin, which lay deep within the Soviet zone: each of the Allies controlled part of it. The onset of the 'Cold War' led to the collapse of these arrangements: in 1949 Russia turned its zone into the German Democratic Republic of Germany. The Western powers, however, remained in Berlin. This was an embarrassment to Russia.

During the 1950s, hundreds of thousands of East Germans fled to the West through Berlin – the worst possible advertisement for Communist rule. Between 1958 and 1961, Khrushchev tried to force the Western powers out of Berlin but they stood firm. In 1961 the Berlin Wall was built to prevent people escaping to the West.

Khrushchev suffered a more important diplomatic setback over Cuba in 1962. Under the leadership of Fidel Castro, Cuba became a CLIENT STATE of Soviet Russia. Khrushchev, believing that he could boost his prestige at the expense of a weak United States' President, ordered the construction of a missile base on Cuba. He was, however, outmanoeuvred by his opponent. The United States imposed a 'quarantine zone' around Cuba. It threatened to sink any ship carrying weapons which entered this zone. Khrushchev was forced to order Soviet ships loaded with equipment for the missile base to turn for home. He agreed subsequently to dismantle the base.

The early 1960s also saw the opening of a rift between Russia and Communist China. The Chinese were as much, if not more, to blame for the split as the Russian leader. Khrushchev, though, allowed himself to be drawn into a slanging match with the Chinese. In the course of this he called Mao Tse-tung, the Chinese Communist leader, a 'worn-out old boot'. His colleagues criticised him for being undignified. They also blamed him because, as a result of the split, Russia lost its position as the unchallenged leader of the Communist world.

Assessment

1 Describe three examples from Khrushchev's domestic and foreign policy (pages 50 to 55) of what **Pravda** had in mind when it spoke of 'hare-brained scheme-making' (Source 16).

2 Describe, and account for, the likely attitude towards Khrushchev in the early 1960s of the governments of the United States, China, Cuba and East Germany.

3 Do you think the reasons why Khrushchev became unpopular among (a) senior members of the Communist Party, (b) Russian writers and artists and (c) Russian factory workers were the same or different? Give reasons for your answer.

4 Why, by 1964, was Khrushchev more admired in the West than he was within Soviet Russia?

5 Do you suppose that Pasternak's view of Khrushchev (Source 15) was typical of attitudes towards Khrushchev within Russia? If not, why not?

6 Why is it difficult to reach final conclusions about the reasons for Khrushchev's downfall?

SOURCE 15

For so long we were ruled over by a madman and a murderer – and now by a fool and a pig.

(Boris Pasternak, Soviet novelist who in 1958 was refused permission by Khrushchev to travel abroad to receive the Nobel Prize for Literature, speaking in the mid 1950s.)

SOURCE 16

The Leninist Party is the enemy...of hare-brained scheme-making, of half-baked conclusions and hasty decisions and actions taken without regard to realities. Bragging and PHRASEMONGERING, bossiness, reluctance to take account of scientific achievement and practical experience are alien to it.

(From Pravda, Communist Party newspaper, 1964.)

SOURCE 17

The feeling that Khrushchev had outstayed his time had rapidly gained ground in the ruling group and far beyond it. Qualities which endeared the former Soviet premier to some people in the West – his incoherence, his clownishness, irresponsibility and unpredictability – increasingly worried and angered many Communists, even those who had supported Khrushchev.

(Isaac Deutscher, British historian and commentator on Soviet affairs, writing in 1964.)

Downfall

In 1964 Khrushchev was forced into retirement by his Praesidium colleagues. He did not lose office because he was unpopular with the Soviet people at large – though he probably was (see Source 15) – but he was forced out because he had lost the confidence of powerful interests within the Communist Party. Sources 16 and 17 show that his manner and style, as well as the failure of many of his policies, were responsible for his downfall.

Khrushchev tried to make Communist rule acceptable to the Soviet people and succeeded in bringing about modest improvements in their living conditions. His reforms were, however, limited in scope. Only under Mikhail Gorbachev, more than 20 years later, were attempts made at fundamental reform. These were to shake the Soviet Union apart.

Gorbachev's Russia, 1985 to 1991

Brezhnev, Andropov and Chernenko

Leonid Brezhnev dominated Soviet politics between 1964 and his death in 1982. The Brezhnev era was one of conservatism and stagnation which saw no major attempt at reform of the USSR's planned economy. Economic growth was sluggish. Spending on the armed forces was high. Corruption was widespread. However, there was some improvement in living standards.

After Brezhnev's death, the Soviet Union was ruled briefly by Yuri Andropov (1982 to 1984) and Konstantin Chernenko (1984 to 1985). Andropov was a would-be reformer and Chernenko was a cautious Brezhnevite, but neither was in office long enough to make much impact. Chernenko's successor as general secretary of the Communist Party was the 54-year-old Mikhail Gorbachev (see FOCUS below).

Gorbachev's revolution

Gorbachev presided over a revolution in relations between the USSR and other countries and in the process won world-wide acclaim. In 1989 Soviet troops began to withdraw from eastern Europe: the USSR's satellite states were left free to decide their own futures. The demolition of the Berlin Wall was followed by the reunification of East and West Germany in 1990. A major nuclear disarmament treaty was agreed with the USA in 1991. The 'Cold War' came to an end.

At home, Gorbachev's main aim was to make the Soviet economy more productive and prosperous. In 1986 and 1987 he put forward his policy of 'perestroika', meaning economic restructuring (Sources 18 and 19). Gorbachev quickly concluded, though, that his economic programme would not work unless it was accompanied by other changes. He believed that the Soviet people would only work more enthusiastically if the Communist Party were more open and honest with them than it had been in the past. He also decided that the people had to have a bigger say in the way they were governed. Perestroika was therefore accompanied by the policies of glasnost (openness) and democratisation.

Perestroika

Perestroika was an attempt to release people's energies by freeing them from central control. The Law on State Enterprises (1988) left factory managers largely responsible for their own affairs, although the factories were still publicly-owned. The Law on Co-operatives (1988) allowed some forms of privately-owned business to start operating. The planned economy introduced by Stalin became a thing of the past. In Gorbachev's Russia there was a mixture of public and private ownership in the way there had been under the NEP in the 1920s.

Glasnost

The original purpose of the policy of glasnost was to win support for perestroika by exposing corruption and inefficiency

FOCUS ...Mikhail Gorbachev

- Born in 1931, son of an agricultural mechanic
- Trained as a lawyer at Moscow University
- Appointed Communist Party General Secretary in 1985
- Became the USSR's President in 1988
- Resigned from office, 1991

Mikhail Gorbachev differed from his immediate predecessors as Soviet leader in a number of ways. He came to power when he was middle-aged, rather than elderly. He had a university education. He relished foreign travel and meeting people. He had a high profile and highly educated wife, Raisa. These things, together with his honesty, decency and determination to end the Cold War, made him very popular outside the USSR. Inside Russia his initial popularity waned with the failure of his economic policies.

where they occurred. Before long, however, Soviet citizens were seeing and hearing all manner of things previously kept hidden. Banned works of literature, such as Pasternak's *Dr Zhivago*, were published. Government statistics appeared for the first time on social problems such as drug abuse, prostitution and crime. Interviews with Western politicians, including British Prime Minister Margaret Thatcher, were shown on Soviet television. There was more freedom of discussion than at any time since the downfall of Tsarism in 1917.

Democratisation

In 1988 Gorbachev amended the USSR's constitution. A new law-making body, the Congress of People's Deputies, was created. About one-third of its members were to be nominated by the Communist Party, the other two-thirds were to be elected. Candidates representing parties other than the Communists were to be allowed to stand for election. Elections for the new deputies took place in 1989. For the first time since the Constituent Assembly in 1917 voters were able to make a choice between candidates of different parties. In many cases, the Communist Party candidates were defeated.

Another constitutional change that took place in 1988 concerned Gorbachev himself. Before 1988 he had held the position of general secretary of the Communist Party. In 1988 he became executive President of the USSR. He was not elected to this post; he simply assumed it.

◄ **SOURCE 18**
'You won't get far with a sledge-hammer', a poster supporting perestroika by Victor Bunakov, 1988.

SOURCE 19

The starting point of perestroika was the profound conviction that we could not go on living as we were. I have never, not once, regretted the fact that I was the initiator of a sharp turn in the life of our country. A system created according to the rules of brutality and tyranny could no longer be tolerated, not simply from the moral point of view but also from the point of view of the country's basic economic and social interests. It had led the country to a dead end and brought it to the brink of an abyss ... Perestroika was thus vitally necessary: no other means existed for extricating ourselves from the vicious circle into which the country had fallen.

(Mikhail Gorbachev, writing in 1989.)

QUESTIONS

1 *What criticism do you think the poster in Source 18 is making of the USSR's economy before Gorbachev?*

2 *Why do you think Gorbachev believed that the system he inherited could not be tolerated from the moral point of view?*

3 *In what ways do you think Gorbachev's policies involved a 'sharp turn' away from the policies of both Stalin and Khrushchev?*

Why did the Soviet Union collapse in 1991?

In 1991 the Soviet Union and the control of the Communist Party collapsed. Some 'instant' histories of this collapse have already appeared, and several journalists have also written accounts of the last days of Communist rule. There has been little detailed historical research, however, and there is still much to be learnt about Communism's failure. All that can be offered here are some preliminary ideas.

Long-term causes

The policies introduced by Gorbachev were one reason for the collapse of Communist rule. But there were other, longer-term, causes as well. The USSR was an ailing state before Gorbachev came to power. By the 1980s there was no real enthusiasm for Communism among the Soviet people. One important reason for this was the failure of the USSR's planned economy – despite the boasts of Khrushchev (see Source 7 on page 51) and others – to provide its people with high standards of living. Housing was poor, food was in short supply and consumer goods were scarce. Queuing became part of the Soviet way of life (Source 20). From the 1960s onwards, things like television and the opening up of the Soviet Union to Western tourists made Soviet people increasingly aware that life was more comfortable elsewhere.

SOURCE 20

Shopping is an art in Soviet life. It should be: women on average spend three hours a day practising it – before, during and after work. The rules become second nature. First get into the queue before bothering to find out what it is for; if people are queuing then there must be more than macaroni at the far end. Next: never stand in just one queue; the really expert can manage three or more at a time.

(Angus McQueen, British reporter in the USSR, 1989.)

SOURCE 21

Why should the politically well-connected have more comfortable flats, better foodstuffs, special hospitals and even their own cemeteries?

(From a letter published in *Moscow News*, 1988.)

SOURCE 22

What kind of government is it if we can't even get washed?

(A factory worker quoted in *Pravda*, 1989.)

Another important reason for the collapse of Communist rule was corruption. Members of the Communist Party, well under 10 per cent of the population, awarded themselves all sorts of privileges. They lived prosperous lives while others suffered. The kind of resentment this produced can be seen in Source 21.

The failure of perestroika

When perestroika was launched in 1985 people's hopes and expectations were high. By 1991 they were massively disillusioned. For many, probably most, Russians life got worse rather than better. The main reason for this was that factory managers often used their newly-gained independence to concentrate on expensive and profitable products and reduce production of cheap and unprofitable ones. As a result, commodities like soap, washing powder, toothpaste and matches were in short supply (Source 22). Prices rose sharply. Those worst hit were pensioners and others living on fixed incomes. While pensioners struggled some Russians were able to make fortunes trading unofficially on the 'black market'. Among them were organised crime syndicates. Gorbachev appeared powerless as things ran out of control. His popularity slumped.

Nationalism

The Soviet Union, like the Tsar's Russia before it, was a multi-national state. That is it was a country whose population was made up of people of many different nationalities. After 1917 efforts were made to weaken peoples' sense of belonging to a particular nationality and to replace it with loyalty to Communism. Outside the USSR it was often assumed that these efforts had been fairly successful. Events after 1985 proved that this was wrong. Glasnost allowed people to express their feelings openly. The result was an explosion of nationalist feeling which the USSR was unable to withstand.

The first signs of trouble came in 1988. A violent dispute flared up between two of the USSR's constituent republics: Azerbaijan, which was Muslim, and Armenia, which was Christian. Both laid claim to a region called Nagorno-Karabakh. The Red Army was sent in to restore order, but struggled to do so. At the same time, unrest broke out in the Baltic region. The three Baltic Republics – Lithuania, Latvia and Estonia – began to demand their independence from the USSR. In 1990 Lithuania declared it was no longer part of the Soviet Union. The unrest spread from the Baltic to other parts of the Soviet Union. In 1991 Georgia and the Ukraine issued declarations of independence. So, under the leadership of the former Communist Boris Yeltsin, did the biggest of the USSR's component parts, the Russian Federation.

Gorbachev recognised that nationalist movements had such widespread support that there was no point in trying to restore the authority of the USSR by force. Instead he tried to negotiate a new treaty that would link the various republics together. Negotiations were at a crucial state when an attempt was made to overthrow him.

Attempted coup

In August 1991 conservatives within the Communist Party tried to seize power. They claimed that the economy was in chaos and that nationalism was making the country ungovernable. Gorbachev was arrested, but the coup failed. This was not the work of Gorbachev but of Boris Yeltsin. Yeltsin defied the conservatives and public opinion rallied to his support. The coup collapsed after a few days and Gorbachev returned. Yeltsin's prestige soared. He made it clear that he was ready to allow each of the Soviet Union's republics to go its own way. Gorbachev was powerless to stop him. The USSR was dissolved and Gorbachev resigned its presidency. In its place 15 independent states emerged (Source 23), the biggest of them Yeltsin's Russian Federation.

▲ **SOURCE 23**
The 15 independent states that emerged from the old Soviet Union in 1991.

QUESTIONS

1 *In what ways were members of the Communist Party a privileged class in the 1980s?*

2 *Which do you think was the most important short-term cause of Communism's collapse: the failure of perestroika or the growth of nationalism?*

3 *To what extent was Mikhail Gorbachev personally responsible for the collapse of Communist rule?*

4 *'Important economic resources were lost to the Russian Federation when the other republics became independent in 1990–1991.' Making use of Source 23 and of earlier sections of this book, show how far you would agree with this claim.*

Abdicated
Gave up his ruling position, as the Tsar did in Russia.

Aristocrat
Someone whose family has a high social rank, especially someone who holds a title.

Armistice
Agreement between countries who are at war with one another to stop fighting for a time and to discuss ways of making a peaceful settlement.

Armoured divisions
Part of an army made up of tank units.

Arms race
Contest caused by the wish of powerful countries to have more and better weapons than their rivals.

Atheists
People who believe that there is no God.

Belligerent
Hostile and aggressive.

Bourgeoisie
Term used by Karl Marx to describe those who own banks and factories. Sometimes used more loosely to mean 'middle class'.

Cheka
Political police founded in December 1917 in Russia to fight counter-revolution.

Client state
Nation receiving support in the form of money, services and weapons from a more powerful nation.

Coercion
Act of forcefully persuading someone to do something that they do not want to do.

Cold War
State of extreme political unfriendliness between two or more countries although they do not actually fight each other. Used specifically to denote relations between East and West from 1945 to the late 1980s.

Collective leadership
Responsiblility for running the country to be shared between members of the ruling group.

Collectivisation
The setting up of farms operated by groups of people who sell the produce to the state and share the money.

Commissars
Heads of government departments in Soviet Russia.

Communism
Political belief that the state should own and control the means of producing everything, so that all levels of society can be equal because everyone will do as much as they can and get as much as they need.

Communist society
Group of people whose way of life is run on the political belief of Communism.

Comrades
Name for people who belong to the same political group as yourself; used in socialist or communist groups as a form of address, instead of Mr, Mrs or Ms.

Congress
Meeting of Communist Party representatives in Soviet Russia to discuss issues, ideas and policies.

Conscription
Making people in a particular country serve in the forces both in home and overseas campaigns.

Constitution
System of rules which defines the principles on which a state is governed and the rights and duties of citizens.

Consumer goods
Items purchased by the public.

Dissidents
People who disagree with and criticise their government or powerful organisation, especially when asked to do something difficult or dangerous.

Dissolved
When applied to parliament it means the institution is officially ended or broken up.

Freedom of speech
Right to express an opinion, often religious or political, without government interference.

Free market economy
Economic system in which buyers and sellers operate without government interference.

Garrison
Group of soldiers whose job is to guard a town or building.

Genetics
Study of how qualities and characteristics are passed on from one generation to another by means of genes (parts of a cell in a living thing which control its physical features, growth and development).

Haemophilia
Inherited disease, usually affecting men, in which a person's blood does not clot properly, so that they bleed for a long time when injured.

Heavy industry
Industries which produce raw materials like coal, iron and steel which are bought by manufacturers.

Hoarding
Saving or storing things, often in secret, because they are valuable or important to you. This sometimes results in shortages and rising prices.

Indoctrination
Teaching of a particular belief or attitude with the aim that they will not accept any other belief or attitude.

Kremlin
Ancient walled area in central Moscow which in the twentieth century has housed government offices.

Liberals
People with moderate political beliefs who oppose dictatorship and favour a free market economy.

Manifesto
Written statement produced by a group of people, especially a political party, in which they state their aims and policies.

Mausoleum
Building which contains the grave of a famous person or the graves of a rich family.

Orthodox Church
Branch of Christianity, strong in Eastern Europe and Russia, established by a breakaway from the Catholic Church in the early middle ages.

Peasantry
Group of agricultural workers in a country who usually work a small piece of land in a poor country and who are considered to be of low social status.

Phrasemongering
Using fine-sounding expressions.

Police state
Nation in which the government controls people's freedom through the police, especially secret police.

Praesidium
Name sometimes used in Communist countries to describe important committees.

Proletariat
Term used by Marx to describe those who owned no property and who had to sell their labour to survive. Sometimes used more loosely to mean 'working class'.

Propaganda
Information, often exaggerated or false, which is spread by political groups to influence the public.

Purges
Removal from a political party or organisation of all those who do not agree with the leaders.

Renegades
People who abandon the political beliefs they used to have, and accept different beliefs.

Requisitioning
Formally demanding the use of a vehicle, building or food, especially by the army.

Revolutionaries
People who believe in seizing political power by force.

Saboteurs
People who deliberately damage or destroy property, machines, bridges etc. in order to weaken an enemy or as a protest.

Satellite states
Countries or organisations which have no real power of their own but which are dependent on, or governed by, a more powerful country or organisation.

Social classes
Groups of people who have similar incomes and similar ways of life and so tend to group together.

Socialists
People who believe in a set of political beliefs and principles whose general aim is to create a system in which everyone has an equal opportunity to benefit from the country's wealth, usually by having the main industries owned by the state.

Soviet
Elected council in the Soviet Union. Also used to describe someone who belongs or relates to the Soviet Union or to its people.

Steppes
Large areas of land with grass but no trees. Refers specifically to the area stretching from Eastern Europe across the southern Soviet Union to Siberia.

Summit conferences
Meetings at which world leaders, or leaders of a particular group of countries, discuss important matters such as trade, peace etc.

Superindustrialist
Word used in political debates in Soviet Russia in the 1920s to describe someone who believed in very rapid industrialisation.

Terrorism
Use of violence - such as murder, kidnapping and bombing - to achieve political aims.

Tyrant
Ruler who has absolute power over other people and who uses this power cruelly and unjustly.

Visual arts
Things you can look at and appreciate, such as drawings, paintings and sculpture.

Page numbers in **bold** refer to illustrations/captions.

agriculture 8, **19**, 34–35, 39, 43–44, **53**
Andropov, Yuri 5, 56
Armenia 59
army 13, **20**–22, 40
arts 18, 39, 49, 52
atomic bombs 51
Austria **12**, **18**, **45**, 54
autocracy 7, 39
Azeff, Evno 10
Azerbaijan 59

Babel, Isaac 39
Baku **19**, 36, 41
Beria, Lavrenti 38, **50**
Berlin **45**, 52–53
'Bloody Sunday' 5, 11
Bolsheviks 5, 10, 16–25, 30–33, 39
Brest-Litovsk **4**, **12**, **18**, 22, 32
Brezhnev, Leonid 5, 49, 52, 56
Bukharin, Nikolai **32–33**, 38
Bulganin **50**
Bullock, Alan **39**
Bunin 13

capitalism 25, 34
Castro, Fidel 55
censorship 42, 44
Chagall, Marc 18
Cheka 18, 22, 26, 38
Chernenko, Konstantin 5, 56
Chernov, Victor 10
China 48, 55
churches, **42**
Churchill, Winston 23
civil war 18–25, 48
coal **4–5**, **8**, **19**, **36**, 47
collectivisation 28, 34–35, 44, 47, 52
'Comecon' 45
'Cominform' 45
Comintern 29
Communist Party 18, 30–33, 39, 44, 46, 48, 50–51, 55, 58–59
consumer goods 13, 24-25, 50–51, 53, 59
Congress 31, 47, 51–52, 57
Conquest, Robert **46**
Constituent Assembly, 18, 20
Constitutional Democrats ('Cadets') 10, 13, 15, 22
Council of People's Commissars 19, 32,
Cuban missile crisis 5, 52–53, 59

Daily Herald **44**
Daily Worker **43**
Davydovo, battle of 46
de Jonge, Alex 50
democracy 11, 22, 29, 57
Denikin, Anton **21**, **25**
Deutscher, Isaac **57**, **59**

disease 6–7, 14
Djilas, Milovan **45**
Dnieper dam **28**
Duma 11, 14–15
Dzerzhinsky, Felix **22**

economy 34–36, 52, 58
Eisenhower, President 54
Ekaterinburg **4**, 23
Estonia **18**, 59

factory workers **7**, 11, 15, 21, 34–35, 37, 48, 52, 55
famine **17**–18, 24, 35
farming 8–9, 32, 34–35, 42–43
Finland **18**, 21, **45**
First World War 12–15
Five-Year Plans 5, 28, 36–37, 44
food 13–**14**, 17, **24**–25, 50
France 8, 19–21, 22, 40, 48
freedom of speech 10, 29, 56–57, 59
free market economy 38, 58–59

Gagarin, Yuri 51
Germany **5**, **8**, **12**, 15, 17–18, 22–23,28, 38, 42–43, **45**–46, 48, 54
Georgia 32, 33, 59
glasnost 47, 56–57, 59
'glavlit' 18
Gomulka, Wladyslaw 54
Gorbachev, Mikhail 3, 5, 51, 55, 56–59
Gorshkov, Admiral 51
'Gosplan' 36
grain **19**, 34-**35**, 52
'Great Patriotic War' 5,42, 44
great terror 38–39
Guchkov, Alexander **10**, 11, **15**
GULAG camps 4–5, 39, 52

Hill, Christopher **27**
Hitler, Adolf 29, 42–43, 46
Hungary 14, **18**, **54**

industrialisation 32, 34, 36–37, 48–49
industry **4**, 8–9, 18–**19**, 24–25, **36**–37, 44, 50, 53, 56
iron **4–5**, **19**, **36**
Izachnik, Nikolai **25**

Japan 11, 38
'July Days' **21**

Kaganovich, Lazar 32, 48, **50**
Kamenev, Lev **31**–33, 38–39
Kandinsky, Vassily 18
Kaplan, Fanya 26
Karlovich, Augustus **24**
Kazakhstan 4, 52–53
Kerensky, Alexander 15, 20–**21**
Khrushchev, Nikita **4–5**, 46–55
Kiev 14, 17, 41

Kirov, Sergei 38
Knickerbocker, Hubert **35**
Kolchak, Alexander **23**
'kolkhozy' 34, 42, 47
Kornilov, General 21
Kremlin 44, 46
Kronstadt **4**, 24
kulaks 34-35, 47
Kursk **41**, 43, 48
Kutuzov, Marshal 42–**43**

labour camps **29**, 39, 52
Ladoga, Lake **41**, 45
Landau, Lev 39
Laqueur, Walter **27**
Latvia **18**, **45**, 59
Lee, Stephen 27
Lenin, Vladimir **5**, **10**, **16–27**, **28**, 32, 38 48
Leningrad 4, 26, 36–38, 41, 44
Liberals 10, 23
Lithuania **18**, **45**, 59
living conditions 7–9, 11, 51, 55, 58
Lockhart, Robert Bruce **23**
Lvov, Prince 15
Lysenko, T.D. 44

Magnitogorsk 4, 28, **36**
Malenkov, Georgi **50**
Mandelshtam, Osip 39
Martov, Yuly **11**
Marx, Karl 10–**11**
Marxism 3, 16, 29, 38
Masurian Lakes, battle of **12**
mausoleum **26**, 47
Mensheviks 10, 15, 20, 22, 30, 33
middle classes 10–11, **12**, 15, 23
Milyukov, Paul **10**, **13**, 15
Molotov, Vyacheslav 32, 50
Morning Post 27
Moscow 4, **18–19**, 21, 24–**25**, 28, 36, 41–42, 44, 48

Nagorno-Karabakh 59
Nagy, Imre 54
Neivestny, Ernst **49**
'nepmen' **25**
New Economic Policy 18–19, 24–25, 32, 34, 46, 56
Nicholas II **5–9**, 11–**15**
NKVD 38–39
Non-Aggression Pact 40
Novikoff, George **22**
Novocherkassk, **4**, 52

October Revolution 14, 16, 24, 31, 37
Octobrists 10, 13, 15
OGPU 35
oil **4–5**, **36**, 41
'Operation Barbarossa' 40
Orlov, Leonid 25

Orthodox Church 20, 42, 52

Pasternak, Boris 55, 57
peasants **8**–11, 13–14, 21–25, 34–**35**, 42, 44
perestroika 56–58
'permanent revolution' 31, 33
Petrograd **5**, **7**, **12**, **14–16**, 18–**21**, 24, 26, 30–31
Poland 17–18, 22, 34, 40, **45**, 48, 54
'Politburo' 30–32, 44
population 6, 8, 18, 23, 43, 51, 53
Potemkin 10
poverty 8
Pravda 26, 32, 55
propaganda 35, 37, 44–45
Provisional Government 15, 20–21
Pskov 12, 14
purges 5, 38–39, 44, 48–49

'Rabkrin' 30
Radek 38
railways **8**, 14, 21
Rasputin, Grigory 12–13
Red Army **22**, 24, 33, 38, 41–42, 45, 48, 56, 59
'Red Guards' 35
'Red Terror' 22–23
religion 18, 42, 52
requisitioning **24**–25
resisters **42**
Riga, Treaty of **12**, 18, 22, 40
'Right Opposition' 32–33, 47
Rodchenko, Alexander 18
Rodzianko, Mikhail 13
Romania **12**, **18**, **45**
Russian Social Democratic Labour Party 10
Rykov, Alexei 32–33

St Petersburg 4, 11, 19
satellite states **45**, 48, 54, 56
science and technology 18, 28, 39, 44, 51
Scott, John **34**, **36**
Second World War 28, 40–43, 47–48
'seksots' 39
'show trials' 38
Siberia 4, 22–23, 30, 34, 50, 52
Simbirsk **4**, **18**–19
Smith, Redell **45**
Snow, C.P. **39**
'Socialist legality' 52
'Socialist Realism' 45
Socialist Revolutionaries 10, 15–16, 20, 22, 26
Socialists 10, 23, 31
soldiers 13–15, **20, 42**
Solzhenitsyn, Alexander **52**
'sovkhozy' 34
sovnarkhozy' 53
Stakhanov, Alexei **37**
Stalin, Josef 3–5, 19, 27–50, 53
Stalingrad **4**, 29, **41**, 43–44, 49
steel **8**, **19**, **36**, 53
Stolypin, P.A. 9, 11
summit conferences 46, **48**, 54

Tannenberg, battle of **12**
tanks **40**–41, 43, **54**
Tomsky 32–33
'troika' 31–32
Trotsky, Leon 19, 21–23, **30**–33, 38–39, 47
Tsar **6–7**, 10, 11–14, 19
Tse-tung, Mao 55
Tsushima, battle of 11
Tupolev, A.N. 39

Ukraine 4, 18, 22, 41–42, 48, 59
United Nations 48–**49**
United States 20, 42–43, 48, 50–51, 54–55
uprisings and protests 11, 52, 59
Urals **4**, 34, 36

Vavilov, Nikolai 39
'Virgin Lands' scheme **4**, **52–53**
Vlasov, Andrei 42
Voroshilov, Kliment **50**
Vyshinsky, Andrei 38

wages **14**
'War Communism' 18, 24–25, 27
Warsaw **12**, 22, 54
White Russians 17–**19**, 22–**24**
Witte, Sergei **9**
women 6, 14
Wrangel **19**

Yagoda, Genrikh 38
Yeltsin, Boris 59
Yezhov, Nikolai 38
Yudenich **19**, **23**
Yugoslavia **45**, 48

zeks 52
Zhdanov, Andrei **44**–45
Zhukov, Marshal 41, 43–44
Zinoviev, Gregory **31**–33, 38–39

Every effort has been made to contact the holders of copyright material but if any have been inadvertently overlooked, the publishers will be pleased to make the necessary arrangements at the first opportunity.

The publishers would like to thank the following for permission to reproduce photographs on these pages:

T = top, B = bottom, R = right, C = centre, L = left

The British Library 11,40; Victor Bunakov/Sovietsky Khudozhnik Publishers 57; Camera Press 54B, Russian Pictorial Collection/Hoover Institution Archives 17B; Hulton Deutsch Collection 25; Imperial War Museum, London 43L; David King Collection 10, 13, 15B, 16, 17T, 23, 24B, 28, 29B, 30L, 31, 32T, 34, 35, 38T, 40, 41L, 44, 50; David Low (Russian Sketchbook) Solo Syndication/C.S.C.C., University of Kent at Canterbury 26B; David Low (Evening Standard) Solo Syndication/CSCC University of Kent at Canterbury 45; Marx Memorial Library 3T, 26T; Novosti 3B & R, 6, 7, 8, 9, 14, 19, 20, 21, 32B, 36, 37, 41T & C, 42, 43R, 49T, 53, 56; Popperfoto 15T; The Punch Library 54T; Thames Television 29T. Cover: Robert Harding Picture Library.

The author and publishers gratefully acknowledge the following publications from which written sources in this book are drawn:

Octobrists to Bolsheviks: Imperial Russia 1905–1917 by Martin McCauley, reproduced by permission of Edward Arnold (Publishers) Limited; *The USSR since 1945* by E Campling, published by B T Batsford Ltd; *Khrushchev Remembers*, E Crankshaw (ed.), published by Andrew Deutsch Ltd; *Outstanding International Press Reporting* Volume 1 by H D Fischer, published by Walter de Gruyter & Co., Berlin; *The February Revolution: Petrograd 1917* by Tsuyoshi Hasegawa; *Stalin and the Shaping of the Soviet Union* by A de Jonge, T Wilson (ed.) and *Hitler and Stalin: Parallel Lives* by Alan Bullock, HarperCollins Publishers Limited; *Conversation with Stalin* by M Djilas, Rupert Hart-Davis, an imprint of HarperCollins Publishers Limited; Alexander Solzhenitsyn's *The Gulag Archipelago*, Harvill, an imprint of HarperCollins Publishers Limited; extracts from *British Documents on Foreign Affairs*, J Bourne and D C Watts (eds), Crown copyright and reproduced with the permission of the Controller of Her Majesty's Stationery Office; Hodder & Stoughton for Christopher Hill extract from *Lenin and the Russian Revolution*; *The Great Terror* by Robert Conquest and Russia at War by E Karpov, published by Hutchinson; *Russia in Change, 1870–1945* by J Robottom published by Longman Group Ltd; *Marxism After Marx* by D McLellan 2nd edition, The Macmillan Press Ltd; *Nikita Sergevich Khrushchev, 1991* by Martin McCauley; *The European Dictatorship, 1918–1945* by Stephen Lee and *Russian Writers and Soviet Society, 1917–1918* by Ronald Higley, published by Methuen & Co.; *Endurance and Endeavour: Russian History 1812–1992* by J N Westwood (4th edition 1993) by permission of Oxford University Press; three tables from *An Economic History of the USSR 1917–1991* by Alec Nove (Allen Lane The Penguin Press, 1969, Third edition 1992) © Alec Nove 1969, 1972, 1976, 1982, 1989, 1992; Red Star Press for *J V Stalin, Works*; *Khrushchev Remembers*, E Crankshaw (ed.), Sphere Books, an imprint of HarperCollins Publishers Limited; *A Documentary History of Communism* Vol. 1 by R V Daniels, I B Tauris & Co. Ltd Publishers; *Nazism 1919–1945, Volume 3: Foreign Policy; War and Racial Extermination*, J Noakes and G Pridham (eds), University of Exeter Press; *The Fate of the Revolution* by Walter Laqueur and *Russia in Revolution* by L Kochan, published by Weidenfeld and Nicholson; *Source Book for Russian History* by Verdansky et al., Yale University Press; from `Red Empire' a Granite Production for Yorkshire Television Ltd.

Published by Collins Educational,
77–85 Fulham Palace Road
London W6 8JB
An imprint of HarperCollins*Publishers*

© HarperCollins*Publishers* 1995

First published 1994
This edition published 1995

ISBN 0 00 327014 9

Series planned by Nicole Lagneau
Edited by Stephen Attmore and Louise Wilson
Cover designed by Peartree Design Associates
Book designed by Sally Boothroyd
Picture research by Celia Dearing
Production by Mandy Inness
Artwork by Julia Osorno pages 8, 35, 51;
    Hardlines pages 12, 18, 19, 40, 45; Jillian Luff page 59
Printed and bound in Hong Kong